T0285392

Also by David Coggins

The Optimist

Men and Style

Men and Manners

THE
BELIEVER

A YEAR IN THE FLY FISHING LIFE

DAVID COGGINS

SCRIBNER

New York London Toronto Sydney New Delhi

Scribner
An Imprint of Simon & Schuster, LLC
1230 Avenue of the Americas
New York, NY 10020

First Scribner hardcover edition April 2024

Scribner and design are trademarks of Simon & Schuster, LLC

Simon & Schuster: Celebrating 100 Years of Publishing in 2024

For information about special discounts for bulk purchases,
please contact Simon & Schuster Special Sales at 1-866-506-1949 or
business@simonandschuster.com.

The Simon & Schuster Speakers Bureau can bring authors to your live event. For more information, or to book an event, contact the Simon & Schuster Speakers Bureau at 1-866-248-3049 or visit our website at www.simonspeakers.com.

Manufactured in the United States of America

1   3   5   7   9   10   8   6   4   2

Library of Congress Cataloging-in-Publication Data has been applied for.

ISBN 978-1-6680-0471-5
ISBN 978-1-6680-0470-8 (ebook)

Some of the names have been changed.
All the fishing stories are real.

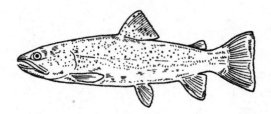

CONTENTS

ix

CONTENTS

THE BELIEVER

INTRODUCTION

A MIDPOINT

I'm halfway through my life. This bracing metric puts time in perspective: A clear, well-defined *before* giving way to a symmetrical, even poignant, *after*. The long view no longer looks so long. I'm forty-five, or I was when I began this book. And it's true that I've been making this dramatic declaration for a few years now, giving the equation an interpretive flexibility, like the message you read in a fortune cookie.

A good part of my life's first half has been given over to fly fishing. I learned to fish on the lake at our family's cabin in Wisconsin. Then I got serious and started driving west to the great rivers in Montana. Once arrived, I made a fool of myself which I accepted as part of a long, even noble, process. Back then everything felt new and I loved those road trips—the landscape, the water, the trout, the dive bars, the sense of freedom. Discovering the world comes easy when you're young and don't mind sleeping in motels where the television is chained to the wall.

Getting older turns out to come as a surprise, which is mildly embarrassing. My beard has turned many shades of gray, and I've started to discover wayward eyebrows that I used to associate with Scotsmen striding the heath with their deerhounds. I'm shocked that the paper edition of the *New York Times* no longer costs a quarter (it's now $4, as it happens). I remember when phones had cords, planes had ashtrays, and fax machines were an object of fascination (though to me they still are).

But it's more than that. I feel a sense of my own obsolescence. My favorite bars are now closed. My favorite bands now dis-banded. Most of my friends have left Manhattan. They discuss prestigious preschools. One bought a lawn mower. This all feels very adult. I'm not among the ranks of homeowners, myself. In fact, until recently my apartment had one closet.

I still set aside time to fish. Some might say a lot of time. Occasionally I meet a person who finds my fishing obsession interesting. In my experience this doesn't last long. That's particularly true when it comes to matters of the heart. Until my darling girlfriend moved in with me, my fishing life remained a relative abstraction to her. In close quarters, however, my devotion to the piscatorial arts began to intrude upon household harmony.

How much you fish changes, like so many things, once domestic obligations enter the equation. How could it not? Fishing, which had signified an individualistic streak, now implies a lack of commitment to our shared life. If we start a family then, well, we know how *that* ends. Fishing moves down the list of priorities and might be left off it entirely. Other things come into focus. I now admit that, yes, the trunk of my car could function as more than my own exclusive fishing storage. It's been devoted to angling essentials for so long I forgot it could be used for anything else. I've also reassessed why I go fishing in the Bahamas with men my father's age, instead of relaxing on the beach with somebody I'd actually like to see in a bathing suit.

Angling, considered in this light, is no longer seen in the independent Thoreauvian tradition. It might, possibly, looked at in a certain way, be considered a distraction. But a distraction from what? That fishing is secretly the primary focus and everything else is a distraction does not go over well at the dinner table.

So I've been thinking about time. When you have a lot of time it's not something you think much about. When you realize there's less time, things unfortunately start to move more quickly. Fishing has a specific relationship to time.

For many of us, the sport operates in opposition to our so-called real lives. Quarterly tax payments (did I remember to pay those?), meetings, interviews, what makes us, in theory, *productive members of society*. To fish properly you need time. Money helps. But you can get around that if you're strategic. Time is the thing. And there's no way to avoid the friction that fishing seriously means you're leaving people behind while you're on the water. People who, when you go salmon fishing in the snow, think you've possibly lost your mind.

That fishing exists outside professional duties recommends it. While fishing I can, for a time, ignore deadlines, conference calls, and fandom of my tragic sports teams. I am, in the best sense, out of reception. Except I'm more connected to what's around me—the shadows on the water, the speed of the clouds, the changing of the light—than at any other time.

Fishing, if we allow it, becomes an antidote to the modern world's focus on the collective present moment. We're updated on developing stories, held hostage to the scroll, the chyron, the feed, the notifications. Everything is endlessly suspended in real time and there's no chance to reflect. Nobody gets their news from the newspaper anymore (even for $4). Once it's printed, something else is already happening. Forget writing a letter, you might as well start a fire with two sticks.

When you travel to fish, this changes the equation. The first thing to do is establish an advance position on the calendar. Wear something three times and it becomes what the fashion rags call a *signature look*. All white, nautical stripes, a novel hat, whether it's good or bad people will recognize it. Similarly the angler must stake out his territory. Go to Patagonia in January once and people think it's indulgent. Ignore them. The second time they come to terms with it. The third time they expect it. They know you fly to Buenos Aires after New Year's—this is *your thing*—and they may roll their eyes but they know you're unavailable for dinner parties and christenings.

While loved ones must be briefed on your long-term plans, fishing remains, to a large degree, a secret life. Actors, athletes, mayors, marines, short-order cooks, high-stakes gamblers, priests—these professions can only be understood when you're on the inside. Only another actor will ever understand the humiliation of forgetting your lines on stage. We're not winning Tony awards here, but only another angler can truly appreciate the joy of catching a two-foot trout on a Blue Wing Olive, a fly smaller than a chocolate chip. Or, conversely, the pain of losing an Atlantic salmon that you've fought all the way to the shore before it snaps the leader and breaks your heart.

Yes, angling can become a full life. And a way to measure a life. The seasons, the years, the people you've fished with, those who patiently taught you, who have moved on to the trout stream in the sky. Now, to your surprise, you are the one who teaches other people. You hear truisms (as far as there are truisms in angling) pour from your mouth as you look upon your charges. *Rod tip up!* you yell, when they have a fish on the line. *Keep the pressure on!* you bellow, like a raving lunatic. This all subsides in a wave of euphoria when they succeed. I have, to my surprise, gotten misty eyed when friends have, with my help, caught their first fish on a fly.

Is this because I want them to be happy? Because I want them to understand, in some small way, what's hijacked my life? I don't know. Somebody yelling how to land a fish is not part of the platonic ideal of the sport. But the undiluted smile on their face when they've landed their first trout sure is.

At some point you ask how you ended up here. I'm not sure if this happens to Deadheads at their hundredth show. Or if people ask why they're in the front row at WrestleMania with their face painted. You made some decisions way back when and they stuck. You had a chance to take the off ramp but you kept going. You made it to Las Vegas and placed the big bet. Now you're on the far side of the world trying to get a trout to take a fly, and if it doesn't you might melt down. Catch the fish and you're a genius, and if you don't you ask *Whose brilliant idea was this again?*

When did fishing simply become part of your life? You can't even remember any more. Now you ask when might it no longer be part of your life. Being a couple, having kids. Fishing becomes a suit that moves to the back of the closet—it doesn't fit anymore. Whether that all plays out, you still ask the questions. Or I did anyway. My girlfriend moved in, then COVID arrived and my small apartment felt infinitely smaller. A global pandemic focuses the mind. The outside world seems big and far away. When the lockdown ends, you swear you're going to live more robustly.

As that drama wound down, I vowed to make my way to the places I had always wanted to fish. And that's what I did.

A fishing trip—the phrase still sparks a glimmer of excitement—can be fateful and comical. There's serious, oh so serious, planning for an effort that inevitably contains a healthy dose of ineptitude. This careful planning, sadly, only slightly diminishes the odds for unforeseen humiliations, what Thomas McGuane memorably called *the most dire possible clownage*. Beyond the rain, ornery fish, and an obscure, indestructible strand of local mosquito that doesn't even have a name, there's what's charitably classified as user error. This includes, but is not limited to, shoddy casting, creaky reflexes, and dubious tactical decisions. Then, after all that, there are a couple of jerks fishing in our remote and secret spot: *I thought we were the only jerks who knew about this spot!*

Still, I like to plan trips and like to be asked to join them. Sometimes there's a last-minute emergency the canceler deems even more important than fishing. This fateful moment reveals the priorities and character of all involved. Once the canceler is out, possibly for good, he can't really be trusted again. In his absence I'm called upon to step in at the last second. I don't ask questions and don't need reasons. Like a true angling hero, I reschedule meetings with the vaguest excuses and pack my bag.

Don't ask me to join a fishing trip if you don't mean it. I'll say yes. *British Columbia for steelhead with people I barely know?* Terrific, when should I get there? In the past I would just book a flight, but now I can't simply say yes. I have to run it by my people, which is really a committee of one. I try to formulate a sound explanation and believe the best approach is a slow reveal.

So I have a chance to go fishing in Canada, I tell my beloved. This is good, this leaves open the possibility of a brief trip north across the border—New York to Canada is closer than you think. Well, British Columbia is not closer than you think, unless you live in southern Alaska. *Oh nice, with who?* This innocent question is a little dicey. *Some new friends, you haven't met them.* (Some are so new I haven't met them myself.) This was my first mistake: *New friends* can be a dubious category—they arrive, unvetted, with ideas that enter my impressionable mind. Lacking discipline I find that I've agreed to a trip as the last drink is poured.

Details emerge, like implicating evidence in a trial. I wait before confessing that I will be heading three time zones west. *How long is the trip?* I've predicted this question and am ready. *Well we're fishing for five days.* Technically accurate, but not really providing the whole picture since there will be an overnight in Vancouver. This night and another one, yet to be mentioned, on the way back, are what one friend calls *Associated Days*, devoted to travel and routinely ignored by the angler. *Associated Days* should not be discussed, nor exact financial outlays, which can be considerable. Itemization isn't helping anybody here. Flights, licenses, hotels, guides, tips, a new reel, a new backup reel—final figures shouldn't be explored deeply. Like disclosing the black ops budget, the math just aids hostile interests.

I make my case: *We'll fish the Skeena River!* The majestic Skeena, the noble steelhead, the exquisite British Columbia landscape, like a rainforest—these details fail to make an impression. Now she recites the facts back to me: *So you're going across the country for a week with people you barely know to try to catch a fish that may not even be there?*

Well, when you put it that way. I consider mentioning the Skeena's wonderful tributaries, but using the word "tributaries" during an argument means you're losing that argument. The universe won't suffer if I don't catch a steelhead, yet I feel that I'll suffer. Last year it rained, apparently, but we think this year will be better. Everybody is excited. She asks: *How do your friends know what the weather will be?*

Good question.

In a perfect world you would trust an angler more than a senator. Sadly, that's not always the case, which is even more alarming when you consider who's in the Senate. Of course, the audience most suspicious of anglers is fellow anglers. We view one another with the skepticism of a Mafia goon turned state's witness. But I'd like to establish this as an honest space. Seriously, you can trust me. In these pages, I won't inflate my prowess or exaggerate fish measurements. To prove my good intentions, here are some of my angling shortcomings right up front.

Casting. This seems important. Can't fish without casting. If I'm in a boat, I can cast to a target and feel good about myself. You know what's harder? Making one accurate cast to a large, rising trout twenty-five feet away when wading. I take one cast to warm up, another to the right. Finally I make a deadly accurate cast, an afterthought since the trout has been gone for some time.

Vision. Seeing fish. Again, important. I can struggle to see trout in the current. *Do you see that fish?* the guide asks. My silence indicates that I do not. *Near the pale brown rock?* Another pause. *The moving shadow? A foot off that branch?* He keeps mentioning landmarks—you wouldn't believe how many brown rocks are in this river. Finally I make a cast and he says, *Yes, that's the line. Now just four feet upstream.* A polite way of saying I just cast on top of the fish, which now exits the scene, inevitably as clear as day.

Stealth. They say don't walk right up to the water to see what's going on, you'll frighten the fish. Too often I ignore this, overcome by curiosity. I'll approach a pool expecting trout to be in the best lie and instead one will be farther back, in the slow water, directly in front of where I'm standing. As it flees, I remind myself never to do this again. My specialty.

Those who aren't technically gifted celebrate other qualities of the accomplished angler. We can't compete on superb technique so we focus on intangibles. Like patience. Patience is realizing the last fish you caught was three hours ago and you ask deeper questions about your approach. When the last fish was six hours ago, the questions are too painful. Patience, my child.

Another is *fishiness*. There are fishy flies, fishy parts of a river, and, crucially, there are fishy people. Fishy people have a feeling, born of experience or cosmic intuition. They're uncanny. Regardless of technique, fishy people catch fish, like athletes whose skills aren't measured by statistics. Being fishy requires savvy incongruity. The very real existence of fishiness exists outside analytics. Like everything that matters, being fishy isn't something you claim, it must be named by others.

Perhaps the most important skill is really more of a habit: *Getting on the water*. I admire people who make time to fish. If you don't pursue what you care about, nobody will help you. A long time ago, I graduated from college and moved to Japan. My girlfriend of the time was still in school. When I told her the exciting news, she thought I was joking. I was not. Living in Tokyo was a great decision in my life. She, ultimately, broke up with me, undoubtedly a great decision in her life.

I'm not sure why I went to Japan. Certainly the country appealed to me and remains important to me. I wanted to do something that felt big, or at least unpredictable. Life thought it knew me; I would show life it didn't know me. Whatever life does or doesn't know, the travel habit turned out to be hard to break.

I wrote *The Optimist*, a book about how I fell in love with fishing and the places I traveled to fish. That seems to me now also about being young and then not so young, about how an obsession evolves over time. More and more, being on the water means confronting a changing global climate that affects every place fish live, and always for the worse. That's one reason my fishing trips are charged with a different meaning. They don't express the reckless opportunity they did when I was younger. Now they feel more fleeting, marked, however faintly, with desperation. Each trip might be the last of its kind. Somebody gets a knee replaced. He's out. Another starts a family. So long. It only feels natural to wonder if I'm next.

So, at this self-described halfway point, I felt a sense of urgency—there's less time to live the old way. The French say that delay is the enemy of life. That gives Gallic philosophical cover to go ahead and do whatever you want. But I felt I had unfinished angling business. I still had a chance to visit some good water before I no longer have time for that kind of *diversion* anymore. So I went fishing.

In this year, in the middle of my life, I went out into the world. Far out into it. I wanted to get closer to extreme places of beauty where I could catch fish. Was it desperate? Probably. Inspired? I'm not sure. But the itinerary was no joke: Patagonia, Cuba, Belize, Norway, Spain, Scotland. All overlapping with the insistent return of what Argentinians called the *pandemia*, which, naturally, complicated travel. I was seeking trout, my real love, bonefish (second love), tarpon (developing love), and courting humiliation trying to catch an Atlantic salmon (unrequited love).

A fishing trip is a pilgrimage. Like all pilgrimages it can be single-minded and pure or wild and irrational. Pilgrimages have the clarity specific to the true devotee. That they're mildly unhinged makes them even more appealing. A pilgrimage benefits from simplicity. The line is direct— you hear a calling and you follow the sound. This raises the stakes. What if you don't catch a fish? Then you really become one of the people who says it's not about the fish.

But was it about the fish? That's always the question, isn't it? They say fishing is a metaphor for life—well I don't say that. Sometimes a white whale is just a white whale. I'm still trying to find out. This year of fishing took me across thousands of miles, over mountains, into deserts, on dirt roads, along rivers, and onto seas. I confronted ambition, denial, a desire for something more, which often ended up being far less. There remains a sense of possibility that, in the moment, feels like it can only happen on the other side of the world. Whatever else it is, it's not nothing.

Anglers, at a certain time in their lives, feel called to places. To witness the natural world, to test their skills, to learn something they cannot name. So we head to the great rivers, whose paths are marked across time. We discover another version of ourselves when we're on the water, away from the earthbound side of our lives. The stakes matter only to us, and we cast toward the far shore asking one question: *Do you believe?*

CHAPTER I

ARGENTINA

The Ritual of Return

The Southeast train station is an hour from New York City on the Metro-North line. The sun is bright in a high blue sky. It's January. I'm far from Patagonia. I've just arrived but will be on the next train back to town. The purpose of this brief trip is to collect my waders and boots from my beloved Volvo wagon, which sits under a thin layer of snow in the long-term lot. Clinically speaking, this isn't rational behavior. I accept that. Fly fishing isn't rational. Patagonia isn't rational either. I love to fly fish and love Patagonia, does that make me irrational as well?

Why leave my car at a train station and not in the city where I live? I'm glad you asked. I have a system, which I admire for its tactical brilliance, where I leave my car outside the city. No lots, no bridges, no alternate side parking madness. I relax, take the train from Grand Central, read the *New Yorker*, pay a little to park, and then drive to wherever I'm fishing. Look who's rational now.

This short visit to turn around and take the next train back is extreme even by my standards. My system didn't quite account for this. That's the problem with systems — they solve a problem you know exists, not the one you don't expect. For reasons of space, logistics, and domestic tranquility, most of my fishing equipment resides in the car rather than our concisely proportioned apartment. I should have brought everything down when I was here last month. But there's a moment of idiocy on every fishing trip and I hope to get this one out of the way ahead of time.

In a few days my friend Markley and I are flying to Buenos Aires and on to Patagonia to tour of some of the bluest rivers on earth. We'll be on the road for almost a month. Even in the empty lot I feel the thrill of undiluted purpose and barely contained madness that only fishing inspires in me. I'm ready to head south.

• • •

"What do you want to get out of this?"

The question is disarming. Markley and I are in Midtown Manhattan preparing for our trip. For a discreet man he can get right to the heart of the matter. I'm embarrassed I don't have a good answer. Illumination or something.

I'd like a unifying theory that doesn't sound like the slogan for a new kind of kombucha. Everything that comes to mind feels self-aggrandizing. *I want to understand Patagonia* sounds pretentious because it is pretentious. It's impossible anyway. Hitchhiking across Patagonia on the trail of Bruce Chatwin is a young man's game. I'm too old for that. And I don't want to be on the road anyway; I want to be on the water.

This is a return engagement. I first visited Patagonia almost twenty years ago, landed a few trout but didn't bathe myself in angling glory. I now realize the guides took pity on my amateurism. This stings. You have to start somewhere but now it's easy to see how much I didn't know. In the moment, I'm embarrassed to say, I thought I was doing fine. I'd like to say that was the last time that happened. Patagonia turned out to be the main attraction. I fell in love with the landscape, the guides, the gauchos, the asados, the Malbec, the rivers, and the trout.

Many people fall for Patagonia. Butch Cassidy, of course, who fled the law, rode down and stayed. They said the land reminded him of his Utah home. Bruce Chatwin came, met the Welsh, and made his name. Reading Chatwin when I was young mesmerized me. I wanted to lead a life that took me out into the world, that took me to Patagonia.

Since my first trip as a wayward idealist, I've returned a number of times, caught some trout I remember well and lost some I'd rather forget. But I've never caught *the* fish. I was never quite up to speed. No more. This will be my longest trip, covering the most miles, with the most days on the water. I'm ready for luck to be on my side. I'm excited. What's more thrilling than fishing from mountain streams beneath the Andes down into the great rivers in the desert steppe?

I can't admit to Markley that I want to catch this large trout. That's a bad omen. Aim high and the fishing gods will shake their heads at your ambition and mete out a historic combination of gale-force winds and severe downpours that leaves guides saying, *I haven't seen this in thirty years.* Then they'll toss in some proximate lightning for good measure. Some climb Mount Everest because it's there. The fish I want to catch, far too often, *isn't* there. So I'm setting out to catch a trout worthy of the surroundings and be connected with Patagonia's historic landscape. Delusions of grandeur? You better believe it.

I'm searching for a fish that you can only catch in Patagonia. In the traffic of Midtown this seems improbable. But Patagonia makes people dream big dreams even when they know better, *especially* when they know better. As Nicholas Shakespeare wrote in his Chatwin biography: "In Patagonia, the isolation makes it easy to exaggerate the person you are: drinkers drink; the devout pray; the lonely grow lonelier, sometimes fatally."

He might have added that anglers become even more possessed on the legendary water. Patagonia is the heroic background for long-shot fantasies and believing in something ridiculous is our specialty. Otherwise, what's the point? This is particularly true when the trip still exists in its platonic state, full of possibility, before the wind, the highly selective trout, and all the variables of fishing enter the equation.

Traveling a great distance to fish means facing the threat of coming up short. The potential to bomb out heightens everything. One good fish and you have a story that will bore your friends forever. Or you can take it easy and enjoy the fishing. I've done that before, but this feels different. We'll be there too long, with too many chances. I feel that this may be, I'm afraid to say, *my moment*. That talk puts me on the agenda for the next meeting of the angling gods.

Markley judges grandiose fishing designs. When we're in the Catskills he likes to catch wild trout the size of a hot dog bun. Markley's fished his entire life; it runs in the family. He's not greedy and never complains, good traits for any friend, but especially an angling friend. Markley believes the sport should be hard and skill should be rewarded, which plays to his strengths. He claims, and I'm not sure I believe this, that catching fish is incidental, like he's a goddamn Buddhist monk.

Packing for a fishing trip still excites me. I hope that never changes. Anticipation is inextricably tied to angling; it's the motivation behind every cast. Being well prepared builds confidence in the heart and soul of a man. He considers himself ready for any condition he might confront in Patagonia, all while sitting in the comfort of his Manhattan apartment.

After consulting Argentinian weather reports that will long be out of date, I commit to a healthy array of khaki shirts, a layer of rain gear, and my trusted angling cardigan (oddly this sweater hasn't caught on beyond literature professors in Dirk Bogarde films). I imagine more potential conditions and a few flannel shirts enter the equation. Then I say *To hell with it* and decide to pack a second bag. The second bag implies thoroughness but is, in fact, sloppiness. In my civilian life I'm a concise packer—I receive a strange thrill from bringing less than I need. Packing light is a sign of a well-edited mind. Not this time.

There are rods, reels, waders, boots (straight from Southeast station), and a deep selection of flies. I include my *Maneuver X* box, which I refer to in times of angling need. It's full of mysterious flies, some so small and obscure I have no idea what they're called, that represent the last chance before completely giving up hope.

Markley takes a different approach. He writes breezily: *I'm perfectly happy to improvise and not always have exactly the right thing.* What's this? Markley doesn't want *exactly the right thing?* I read his message again with growing alarm. What's going on here? *Not the right thing? This* is madness. *Not the right thing?!* This won't do. If I fail, I want to fail with *exactly the right thing.*

When cooking, I don't need Himalayan sea salt harvested by humanitarian poets or first press olive oil with a label covered with wildlife drawings. But fishing is fishing.

Anglers need to feel that by choosing the correct fly then we're closer to solving the eternal questions. If it turns out that we can solve them with any default option, with *not the right thing*, then, we fear, there's less strategic genius going on, and we can't have that. If fishing is random then how can we be brilliant?

Markley doesn't see a specific situation that needs to be resolved. Having the right thing implies that one fly provides a solution, a fish, an endgame. Markley takes a broader view. This is not about one fly. We should respond to what we see with the best of what we have and enjoy ourselves. In short, we should relax. Interesting idea.

I still need the illusion of control. This illusion has a number. At the airport my duffel bag weighs in at an ice-cold thirty-five pounds. Disgraceful. The second bag is lighter, the way people's second weddings are smaller, out of mild embarrassment. I tell myself this is the weight of a proper expedition. A big trip deserves a big bag. I hope I'm right.

On the overnight flight to Buenos Aires I watch *Bullitt*, with Steve McQueen, who's unsmiling as ever. Whatever else he did, Steve McQueen really supported the corduroy jacket, a good legacy. I feel like Steve would have approved of my angling cardigan. At one point he declares "Time starts now," and you really believe him. We're flying south, the beginning of a year of fishing. A big year. It's all in front of us.

Time starts now.

•   •   •

Buenos Aires is one of the world's great unhurried cities. We arrive in a heat wave, so there's even less hurry. This sense of ease encourages us to take our time when we stop in vintage stores, sit at the bar for a Quilmes, or admire the architecture as we walk the old streets.

The historic Café Tortoni has a small tango theater in one back room and a pool hall in another. When a beautiful place has a menu in eight languages, you know its best days are behind it. But it's good to escape the heat and imagine the old feeling. We visit Arandu, the store for horse riders, polo players, and the people who love them. The dark wood walls are lined with riding boots, leather saddles, white helmets, woven belts, large knives, larger knives, and other accoutrements for the country gentleman. There's a culture to the *estancia* life, even if the life remains a dream to most.

People walk their dogs down the streets in Recoleta outside stately apartments with balconies covered in winding plants. We sit outside a café near an old *ombú* tree, which looks like an immense umbrella. I visit the cigar store where you can get a good rum though it's too hot today. Knowing their clientele, they mark up the cigars a healthy amount. I buy a few anyway, as I always do.

Back in Soho Palermo, the heat subsides, and people come onto the streets. We have a leisurely dinner outside El Preferida, a well-loved restaurant in a pale pink building on a popular corner. *Porteños* adore ice cream (and sweet things in general), and El Preferida has remarkable gelato and it seems rude not to try it. It's good to be in Buenos Aires as the sun goes down.

We stroll back to the Jardin Escondido, our hotel with an inviting courtyard garden. The rooms are large, tiled, cool. Francis Ford Coppola lived here during a film shoot and is an owner. We'll return at the other end of the trip in a few weeks, after the fishing. What stories will we tell? Will they be tragedies? Comedies? Melodrama?

We step off the plane in Esquel, on the western edge of Patagonia, into a brisk wind coming off the Andes mountains. We've left the heat of the city behind us. The terminal is open and friendly. People are in a good mood as they head off to camp, canoe, or hike. We drive southwest to Trevelin.

I've wanted to stay at the Lodge at Trevelin for years. Run by Patagonia River Guides, this place is hard to crack because regulars return year after year, a good sign. The lodge is at the base of the mountains in the high, green landscape, more lush than the low-lying desert up north.

We're hardly roughing it. Markley said that he was worried Trevelin would offer *too much comfort*. His grandfather camped in a canvas tent and survived on stale Triscuits. At the lodge's request, we sent the terrific chef, Arturo, our dietary preferences, like we're visiting royalty. We're here with passed hors d'oeuvres, for goodness' sake; Markley quickly gets used to it.

Every morning the guides gather outside the lodge — gossiping, smoking, talking tactics, like a team before the coach arrives. They stand in front of a fleet of Toyota Hilux trucks. Each guide has an assistant guide who inflates the raft and breaks it down at the end of the day. The assistant drives the truck to the pull-out, and helps if you're wading. In a few years, if all goes well, he might become a head guide. By that point he'll have no illusions about the job.

The assistant is also responsible for preparing and sharing the yerba maté, the slightly bitter, highly caffeinated herbal tea-like drink you sip out of a dried gourd from a metal straw. Maté is part of social life in Argentina, and there are a variety of rituals, much discussed, about the proper way to prepare, share, accept, and drink it, all of which I never get quite right. Markley sits up front and takes photos of the striking landscape (he was a photographer in a previous life). He and the head guide, Juany, discuss trees and birds, but also engineering and construction (Markley has been known to build a small cabin). I sit in back, come into the morning, watch the landscape pass by, and think about fishing.

We drive toward the Andes and the Rivadavia, where I fished almost two decades ago, and I shudder remembering some of my farcical maneuvers. There's no way to forget the vividly blue water and the mercurial trout. That remains the case. Set in the magical Los Alerces National Park, the Rivadavia runs clear for seven miles between two glacial lakes.

Juany is calm, quiet, and competent. He rows the raft and occasionally stands on the seat trying to see fish ahead of us. The fact that I'm in the front of the boat and should also be able to see the fish is not remarked upon. I cast a Stimulator near a submerged branch, and there's the slightest swirl on the water and the fly is gone. Our first fish. "Take your time," Juany says. Don't rush these strong fish. What I thought was a small trout—the take was so subtle— turns out to be a gorgeous rainbow that fights and fights. In the water next to the boat the fish is silver and clear; a dusty pink streak runs the length of its side.

For our shore lunch, Juany sets up a camp stove and casually makes a terrific, thin steak in a skillet. We sit at a table with a bottle of Malbec and feel good about things. The fishing is slow but we don't mind. We admire amazing copper-colored alerce trees with no bark and expressive, curving branches. Juany points out bamboo-like reeds that come to life every fifty years. Later rain comes and what appears to be hail. Markley catches a nice rainbow on a streamer on the last cast of the day as we enter the lake. Augustin, the assistant, is waiting for us when we pull out on the bank.

Spend any time in Patagonia and you'll drive down dirt roads. You don't know how long a dirt road can be until it's been ten minutes, which feels like half an hour. In Patagonia there are some real teeth rattlers. The drive is always worth it, because you're getting farther away from what's already pretty far out. One boat landing was up, over, and down a hill that was more rocks than dirt. The road wasn't a road at all, just impressions from the tires, and the truck moved at the pace of a person climbing. We just presumed this was safe because they'd done it before. Otherwise it would seem insane.

These days you see construction crews paving roads. Cows wander past the equipment away from their ranches and drivers slow down to avoid them. The country, for better or worse, feels less remote. Better in that you can get more places more easily. Worse in that you're more connected whether you want to be or not.

There's also more cell service and your phone is never safe. Not just your phone but the phones of others, the bane of modern life. One day our drift boat pulled to the bank for lunch where we met other guests from the lodge. We were greeted by the voice of a woman from Texas who was on a video call with a friend from home. *It's amazing down here.* She was rapturous. *I'll be posting photos. Okay, I've got to go they're grilling something.* This pierces my illusion of escape. Chatwin never witnessed anybody on FaceTime.

The next day we drive out into the desert to a spring creek on a large ranch. We stand on the high bank out of view of the fish, and cast hoppers to open areas between the weeds. Make a good cast, twitch the hopper, and trout will ambush the fly in explosive takes. But that's just the beginning, then you have to hurry down to the bank, careful of your footing, and maintain pressure on the line to keep the fish from getting tangled in branches. It's delightful.

From the vast plane a low blanket of gray clouds arrives, visible for miles. There's no wind, not *a drop of wind*, as they say here. We fish in absolute silence in this immense valley. It's eerie. The sense of calm feels fragile and when lightning strikes in the distance we have plenty of room to see it—the echoes of thunder are visceral. Hernan, our guide, who's been genial and relaxed, quickly breaks down our rods and walks briskly back to the truck. This is no place to be during a thunderstorm.

Hernan's surprised. "The Andes stop the rain in Chile" is his poetic explanation about the mountains' effect on weather moving east into the desert. There's nothing green within miles. "The rain here is unusual," he adds. An understatement. It hadn't rained for months and now we're done for the day. A new distinction in the angling weather chronicles.

"In Argentina we have a saying," Hernan tells us, "*when it rains it has to stop raining.*" I wonder if this is reassuring. I share our saying, *When it rains it pours.* And today it does pour, raining more than the entire year. This reminds me of the only time I attended the Kentucky Derby and it rained more than any day in the 150-year history of the race. The women wore plastic bags over their hats.

From the guides we learn things that have nothing to do with fishing. We pass the small graveyard of a man Butch Cassidy may or may not have killed. Augustin tells us the legend isn't real. He didn't kill the man. "My grand grand grandfather lived in the town with Butch Cassidy." Stories of Butch Cassidy swirl around Patagonia and I never know how much to believe. My good impression is based on my affection for Paul Newman's screen version. This is the first tale I've heard from a descendant. "Butch Cassidy was nice," Augustin assures us. "He never robbed the town bank."

• • •

On the drive back we stop in Esquel's old general store. They sell rope by the yard, rolls of fabric (many people here make their own clothes), camp stoves, the baggy pants called *bombachas*, salted almonds, toys, and postcards a few decades old. Whatever you might need before heading to the *mesetas* beyond the city limits.

At the lodge the other guests are eccentric southern lawyers knowledgeable about wine, Alaskan bush pilots, professional mountaineers, mysterious Texans in dark glasses, retired financiers, wives who out-fish their husbands, well-preserved wives who don't fish at all. Fishing lodges throw you all together. At Trevelin, after some good Malbec, you get into the spirit.

Everything is so seamless here. You can get emails, make calls, send videos as if you were right outside New York and not a hemisphere away. Markley regularly checks in back home. I'm less available, I realize. One phone call a week is about my ideal ratio. I presume, selfishly, that it's hers too. But Manhattan apartments are often better when one of the residents is away for a while.

After more fishing and much more eating, we say a wistful goodbye to Trevelin and drive north. On a steep hill we see a forest of araucaria trees, which grow one inch a year. Markley says their seeds at this high altitude are hearty and sought after by his friends back home. Finally, we're met in a parking lot by Facul, another guide. This has all been intricately arranged beforehand. I consider myself a bit of a logistics aficionado. Few would admit such a thing.

Nobody says I like Venice, baseball, and spy novels. But my real love is, and will always be, logistics. Planning provides a feeling of control. More importantly, good planning puts you on the water sooner. And that matters. Facul drives us up the hills toward Arroyo Verde.

The Rio Traful flows for twelve miles, brilliant mountain-blue, between two lakes. On the north side of the river is Arroyo Verde, a majestic, 25,000-acre *estancia*. The matriarch, Meme, lives in Buenos Aires and comes south for the summer. The low-lying stone house is more modest than grand, with a library, walls of sporting prints, and a beautiful old map of the property drawn in blue ink, back when fonts meant something. There are photos, variously faded, of family and friends smiling, sometimes next to startlingly large fish.

This is not a lodge, it's a house, and the house is run by two ladies. They are referred to by the residents of the valley, as *The Ladies*. When we meet them we realize that they are indeed *The Ladies* and can be referred to no other way. The first is Marina, Meme's daughter, with an engaging, gracious manner and an easy smile that immediately puts one at ease. Katrina, whose title is head of hospitality, is a horsewoman, who spent time in the army. A Scot who came to Argentina and stayed, she has a healthy tan, sharp blue eyes, and a theory about how to make a gin and tonic.

Marina apologizes for not being at the house to greet us. "I was in the barns," she says. "I didn't hear you arrived." We're not worried, we're thrilled to be here.

"I was," she searches for a word, "*working* on the male cows."

"Castrating?" Markley asks.

"*Claro*," Marina replies, eyes twinkling.

Marina tells us that after fishing we'll see her for cocktails and then dinner: the late anglers' dream schedule. At Arroyo Verde we feel like guests in a country house. Not everything is about fishing, the siesta is an implicit part of the schedule, which puts matters into perspective.

The Traful is a short drive down a dirt road. In my personal classification system this is a *medium-size* river that runs easily at the bottom of a steep bank. We arrive beneath a large rock—the size of a stack of grand pianos—with a hole through its center. At ten in the morning, we're told, you can look up and see the sun through the opening. We walk along a path above the bank, looking down at the river for trout. Our guide, Andres, stops periodically to assess the water more carefully. I stop to look too. But I'm just imitating what he does, not really a trusted member of the advance team. The water isn't deep, two or three feet, incredibly clear, and we can make out every rock along the bottom.

"*There!*" Andres stares carefully at a rock on the near side of the river. He points to a dark log that, on closer inspection, waves gently in the current. A triangle at one end betrays its true identity: the tail. "*Yes!*" he exclaims, as if the most difficult part of the proceedings isn't entirely in front of us. That's a fish all right. The largest we've seen on this trip. My stomach turns, as it does when I see any big fish. That's a fish that breaks hearts.

We'll see every part of the equation. Good, right? Well, yes. Except not exactly, because you're going to watch the fish move up, possibly quite slowly, to eat your fly. Keep your nerve and don't raise the rod and set the hook too fast, a common mistake. The best anglers I know like to cast to fish they see. They love the challenge. But now it's all right here, I feel a sense of doubt.

We're a few hundred feet away, but we move cautiously down the bank, theatrically slow, like mimes. "Well, give it a shot," Markley says generously. This is why you come to Patagonia. Yet suddenly I feel vaguely ill. This trout will be caught or spooked, there's no third way. Andres and I carefully climb between thorny bushes. Now we're next to the water, close enough to cast.

"He's still there," Andres says. The immense shadow is in front of us. "You see him, right?" There's no way to miss this fish. The angle from this bank is good for a left-handed caster like me. Yet I don't feel lucky. "You want to cast only the leader over the fish," Andres whispers. If the shadow of the thicker fly line crosses over the fish, it will spook.

"Spooking" is a key word here, as it is anywhere fish are sensitive, enlightened, and shy. This happens in clear water. Nobody wants to spook a fish. That can be the result of a variety of foolish behavior, much of it my forte. Fish don't like shadows, which remind them of predators. A long rod and a swinging line are practically designed to cast shadows along the water. We have to be careful.

We're not far from the trout, but the cast has to be perfectly measured. The wind is still up. There's an opening between the branches behind me for my back cast, then a small window where I want to drop the fly. These are close quarters and this is the exact sort of important cast I never practice. Meme's late husband, Monsieur Larivière, the Frenchman with a good name who built this house sixty years ago, was a legendary roll caster. A roll cast doesn't require a back cast—it generates its speed from the surface tension of the fly line moving along the water—and is useful on this river. The fact that I don't have a dependable forty-foot roll cast is not something I care to consider at this delicate moment.

"He's active," Andres says. "Feeding." My stomach is in knots. "If it's a good drift he'll take it." We have a hopper on the surface and a nymph trailing below it, which should run right by the trout. I let out a cast, careful not to catch the trees behind me. Out it goes. Not quite far enough. Better to err on the side of caution. Andres remains calm. "All right. Same line. Five feet further." The fish is still there. Not spooked. My memory of this is quite clear—reinforced by a video Markley sent me afterward.

Later, I watch the video about twenty times. This is what I see: The blueness of the water, the color welcoming, almost tropical. The wind, however, is forbidding and audible. Otherwise the film could easily be silent, understandable to anyone. I cast and the fly lands. Then a large shadow abruptly turns and swims in the opposite direction—the absolute definition of a spooked fish. Quickly, with certainty, the curtain comes down on Act I. There's no Act II. *The play's over. Time to head home, folks, thanks for coming! The star is indisposed in his dressing room and not accepting visitors.* The video continues and our hapless hero turns around and bends to his knees and shakes his head, a defeated man.

Markley says he was filming in case this was a moment of triumph. No doubt he was. But I wonder why he sent the video to me when feelings were still so raw. I keep watching the video as if the outcome will change. The line keeps scaring the fish and the fish keeps leaving. That you could see the shadow of the fish from that distance—Markley was high up the bank—gives a sense of its size. We catch nothing that day and report back to The Ladies about our trout-free afternoon.

"Oh it's windy out there. It's been storming," Marina says over our consolation gin and tonic. "You'll do better tomorrow." This is reassuring, though no doubt she says this to every heartsick angler. Her approach to time is different from ours. Markley and I have only one more day at Arroyo Verde. That's all.

I take an *extremely* cursory glance at the logbook. Fishing logs are a matter of fascination and anxiety, as they list the triumphs of previous guests in excruciating detail. If I told myself plenty of people end up fish-less on the challenging Traful, this log disproves that in black-and-white. At Arroyo Verde a trout must be eighteen inches to even be entered into the log, which puts things into perspective. The perspective is that people catch large fish here then write about it. I run my eye down the page and notice a few entries written by the hand of a child. I tell myself the writing was on behalf of his or her father, not that a twenty-six-inch trout was caught by a ten-year-old. I'm not a competitive person, yet I want to be in this book. I want to be, in a small way, part of the history of this incredible place.

We're not the only guests at Arroyo Verde. Father George, the vicar at Meme's church in Buenos Aires, drove down twenty hours in his small car, as he does every year, to fish, play golf, and visit The Ladies. He's charming and, like Mr. Beebe in *A Room with a View*, arrives just in time for tea. He tells us, in polished English, of his youthful studies in Rome, a beautiful city he found too dingy. He moved to Lausanne for graduate work. Switzerland was cleaner than Rome, yes, but there was nowhere to eat dinner at 10 p.m.

The next day the weather, as predicted, is clear. In the sun it's easier to see fish. Of course that means they can see us. The wind is also down. A good omen. We see a huge landlocked salmon. It's Markley's turn for glory. He casts accurately but the fish barely moves. He puts a cast even closer to its nose, and when it finally flees he's slightly dejected. I wait what I consider to be a respectful amount of time and ask if he wants to see the video, which he knows doesn't exist in any case.

Late in the morning we spot a couple of fish rising side by side. They aren't immense, but still nice. I cast and the near trout, the smaller of the two, takes the nymph as soon as it lands. I fight it quickly and bring it to the bank, not wanting to frighten the larger trout. There's nothing wrong with watching a rainbow trout take a nymph. Andres smiles. A healthy rainbow, wide and pink that appears even brighter in the light. The shutout on the Traful is over. But there's work left to do.

A few casts later the larger fish moves to aggressively

take a hopper. A healthy, strong fish. The sun shines on us and I land a rainbow, nearly nineteen inches. Over the limit for the log. "It's going into the book!" I exclaim. "I don't put a fish in that book less than twenty inches," Andres clarifies, more sternly than I consider necessary. That takes a little vim out of the proceedings. In the log there's a line for the angler's name, the dimensions of the fish, but also for the guide's name. Apparently Andres doesn't want to be associated with the desperation of this 18.5-inch trout. Markley's bemused look implies that this is what happens when you play the numbers game and go down the road of vanity. You get caught up in lesser distinctions and miss the overall. We return to the lodge for lunch in good spirits. We're at Arroyo Verde and the fish are active.

We eat well, drink wine, and after lunch Meme comes and sits with us. She's been working in the garden. "Did you see her dead-heading petunias?" Markley asks in disbelief. In her dark sunglasses and sharp jawline she looks glamorous and intimidating, part 1950s movie star, part cabinet minister. She speaks slowly, but clearly, in English, about the fishing, having been on this river with her husband, and then after him, for over fifty years.

"There are only three or four guides who very well know the river." Andres is one of them, she assures us. "He very well knows the river." She tells us other stories of characters in the valley. "Four aunts—all single—who tended their garden. When they died, all over ninety, all in the same year, their garden died too." The ghosts of Borges are visiting us at Arroyo Verde. Markley and I are dazzled.

"I always say this is my place in the world." She turns

toward the field and speaks again after a time. "Go and have a siesta."

It's late afternoon when we emerge from our rest. We head down to the river and stand on a bank of small stones before a long pool where it's easy to wade. Markley is above me, I fish below. The sun glares on the water's surface so we don't look for fish, they're impossible to see. We cast hoppers and let them swing downstream. When they stop we step down and do it again, covering a lot of water, like salmon fishing. Since we've seen the fish here and know their dimensions this doesn't feel like speculation.

Cast and swing. Another cast, like many before, and the line swings by a half-submerged rock. There's a short, sharp sound, like a vacuum, and the hopper disappears into the wide open mouth of a fish. I'm between mildly prepared and totally shocked. Instinctively, I raise the rod. A good set. "*Yes!*" Andres exclaims, dangerously premature. There's so much to do. The trout, already downstream, heads farther down. Downstream is not where you want a large trout to be. He has the current with him. You can't turn it back toward you. A lot can go wrong.

I hurry after the fish, trying not to let it go farther away. This 2x leader is strong. The bank is flat and shallow, manageable. I'm lucky. I keep pressure on and reel in line every time the trout slows down. After some muscling, the fish is facing upstream toward me. As it gets closer it makes a spectacular leap, doubling over. There's no more guessing. This is a huge fish.

Now, the trout is close and I keep the pressure steady. I back up and lead him to shallow water. Andres is near me holding the net, crouching to keep a low profile. "He's going to run when he sees me," Andres says. That's exactly what happens. I have no choice but to let out line. Emotionally, this is hard to do. We're now further from resolving the situation. I feel a slight ache.

After more reeling, the trout is again opposite me and I can see its entire length in the current. A long, athletic fish. I back up and the trout is tired, close to the bank. Carefully, Andres raises the net under him and lifts a brown trout, bracingly silver in the low evening light. Andres puts his arms in the air and speaks for me, "*Yessssss!*" This is real. We measure him in the net. Streamlined and silver, with stark black spots, no red anywhere. A sleek fish, one that swims distances. On a dry fly. Twenty-six inches. Andres grins and looks at me.

"Now you can put your name in the book."

This is all I want out of my fishing life. To drink tea with Meme and to catch one large trout in the Traful. The sun is setting. I'm done for the day. The landscape, after this success, feels more correct somehow. Maybe I'm more relaxed so I can really appreciate where I am in the world. I enjoy myself. There's nothing left to do. Later, we sit in the living room for Katrina's gin and tonic. Marina says, "We heard you caught your fish." Now I'm at ease. "Yes, it was very nice."

• • •

Later that week, we take the afternoon off from fishing and head to a polo match with The Ladies, who drive down from Arroyo Verde. Fifteen minutes outside St. Martín de los Andes is a green field at the foot of the hills that give way to the mountain. It's pastoral and reassuring, the way fields can be. People park on the grass and sit on folding chairs, as if they're at a children's soccer game. Horses wait for their matches and stay cool in the shade. Every player brings his own horse (though most have more than one). They switch every few minutes, maneuvering from one saddle to another in an exquisite aerial move. One team wraps their horses' legs in red cloth. The horses are beautiful, the players dashing, their families, who watch casually, are handsome.

There's a low-key atmosphere as if this is the most natural thing in the world. We sit with The Ladies at the café and drink beer. They know many of the players, whose families also own *estancias* in the area. Polo, the sport of kings, is far from a democratic pastime. But the speed of the horses is thrilling and the skill of the riders, even to amateurs like me, is astonishing. We take in some of the men's game and then watch the women get ready for their match. Argentinian women riding slowly in their uniforms and tall boots is something worth watching. The Ladies refer to their binoculars.

Andres, who's been sitting with friends by the field, comes over and we drive over to the *Rural*, a country festival with gaucho clothes, food stands, grilling stations, and horse competitions. This is as exciting as the polo match. There are tents devoted to anything you need to cook over fire: grates, tools, Dutch ovens. There are garden stalls where you can buy shovels, picks, and axes in many sizes. Everything you require for the *estancia* you don't have. There are artisanal weavers selling beautiful rugs with prices ratcheted up for *los Yankees*.

There's a small grandstand, ten rows high, made of wood with a ground of dirt where horses are led for the competition. People are drinking in summer, the heat of the day subsiding. We walk around and watch the people who live in the valley. A few polo players come straight from their game in grass-stained uniforms. Andres ends up buying a grill. Fishing, polo, the *Rural*. A good country day.

Return to a place and you have a sense of continuity. You look forward to seeing your favorite guides and beloved rivers, not forgetting the immediate pleasures of Malbec and anything that comes off the grill. You recall previous triumphs and, alas, a few lesser moments. The darting pain of a lost fish is not, I'm sorry to say, easily forgotten. This is the dark side of pursuing large trout. Getting shut out is not ideal. But far worse is catching a big fish and losing it. Knowing this potential devastation, you ask, How badly do you want this trout? You make some clear-eyed decisions and one real gamble.

That gamble takes us to the Limay River, where we camp for our last few days on the water. The Limay flows easily through desert plains beneath red stone bluffs. The level of the river depends on turbines that release water from a dam. Nobody likes the dam, but that's the way it is. The turbines supply energy all the way up in Buenos Aires. The more air conditioners they use in the heat, the more water's released to generate power. You don't want too much water released at once or the river rises suddenly and the fish stay down.

There are many trout in the Limay, some quite large. Markley doesn't care one way or the other. He's enjoying steady action for smaller fish (by Patagonia standards). I'm using a streamer on a sinking line and waiting out one of the migrating brown trout that swim up this river. I feel guilty turning down good fish, but pursuing greatness means I have to be willing to go down with the ship, emotionally speaking.

Catching no trout gives me time to consider the stakes. I think of the trout I lost on the last day of a trip to Patagonia years ago. There was no time to recover. There weren't any life lessons. When you lose a big fish, everything, until the next big fish, feels insignificant. And the next big fish never comes right away. This is why football teams that lose the Super Bowl do badly the following season—nothing measures up to the game they just lost. This isn't an issue for me since I'm from Minnesota and the Vikings have avoided making the Super Bowl since they lost all four they played in back in the 1970s.

The tragedy happens suddenly—where there was once a large fish there is now no fish, of any size. The reasons for failure are not always clear, usually because you don't want them to be. You can't trust the guide because he, in the dreadful aftermath, might not be inclined to say what you did wrong. You need committee hearings with members asking you questions under oath.

Now, is it true that you didn't have the trout on the reel when the fish threw the hook?

Yes, Your Honor.

And is it also true that you had loose line out in the boat at this time?

Your Honor, my counsel has advised me to answer no further questions at this time.

Blame must be laid. And it's painful to identify the easiest target. That's why the angler looks to faulty equipment or some otherworldly interference. At the end of every calamity only one person is holding the rod. Your guide says these things happen. He compares you favorably to some even more unfortunate angler. Then you realize that the next poor bastard who loses a fish is going to be consoled by your pathetic story. Good lord.

If you don't want to lose a big fish, then don't fish for a big fish. That works for a while, but at some point you seek another challenge. That can be a difficult cast beneath an overhanging branch. That can be carefully managing an elegant long drift. Much of angling is doing something you've worked for years to do, and when you finally do it successfully, the fish refuses to do its part. Whether or not you seek that challenge, the challenge will find you.

Markley, as I mentioned, is not competitive. But he is catching fish and I am not. And he has no problem reminding me of my belief in false prophecies. I made my philosophical bed and now I have to sleep in it. He doesn't care about the numbers. He cares that I'm committed to a foolish cause. We've been fishing for more than two weeks in

Patagonia. It's hard to imagine this ever happening again. Still I'm holding out for one last fish. I still believe.

I'm casting streamers on a sinking line so any fish I catch should be large. But I discover a new problem: *La perca*. *La perca* is a river perch. We don't have them in the US. I'm sure these fish will be re-branded one day and called Patagonia silver perch and people will seek them out. Right now they're interfering with the bigger picture.

I'm swinging my line and, bang, it stops. Is this the one? No, I quickly realize, there's barely any pull and it's another perch. Peter, our terrific guide, an accomplished alpine skier, is funny and easygoing. I've fished with him before and it's great to see him again. Markley recalls a Maine restaurant whose sign read: "All the perch you care to eat." That was no doubt a higher number than all the perch I care to catch. We imagine the plural for perch. A quarry of perch. Too positive. A bevy of perch. Not quite right. We settle on a fiasco of perch. And at the moment all I have is the fiasco.

The fiasco grows larger. The perch are all that interrupts my casting and swinging. Otherwise I'm in a zone. I feel good and not that desperate. On the final afternoon I cast, as I have between two and three hundred times, and the streamer swings downstream. Then it stops suddenly with force. As if it hits a rock, or a walk-in freezer, or a Volkswagen, but more animated. This is not a perch.

"*Whoa, whoa, whoa.*" I know right away. I reel in as fast as I can so there's no loose line—I want the fish on the reel. The migrating brown trout here are of a different stature, long, thin, strong. Silver and sleek. The trout is downstream. Peter brings the boat to rest at the side of the river. If I was standing on the bank I would have more room to maneuver and I could lead the fish toward Peter's net. But the bank is too high and it's risky to try to get out of the boat. This is going to take more time.

I keep pressure on the trout. No sudden movements, everything steady. Finally, the trout comes back toward us. We can see its full length opposite the boat. Silver with gold streaks, dappled beneath the surface of the water. "That is a beautiful animal," Peter says slowly, speaking for us all. If you don't respond to a fish like that, then what are you doing here?

We're in a stalemate. Now is the moment for something more. "It's well-hooked," Peter assures me. "Raise the rod when it's near." That sounds easy—in theory it is easy—but a fish can make a final dash when it sees the boat. Raising the rod is a necessary gamble. With this bit of added confidence, I raise the rod, the trout comes closer, and Peter, in an assured motion, slides the net under the fish. It's over.

I would like to say I calmly exhale, but instead I say "Yes" at a high volume. As Peter moves to unhook the fish, the fly falls into his hand. He holds up the streamer and starts laughing. "Well hooked?" Sometimes when the pressure is released the fly comes out on its own. But Peter doesn't say if he actually knew it was well hooked. Did he just want to give me the confidence to try to land it? That's Peter's secret.

The fish is upright in the net and we admire it in the

water. Wide dark back with black spots along a gold flank. *Twenty-seven and three-quarter inches.* We laugh again since an older lady, a tremendous angler, caught a twenty-eight-inch trout yesterday to the chagrin of the more competitive men at camp. "A quarter of an inch short," Peter laughs. "You can round up if you want." There's no need. This fish is perfect as it is.

Back in Buenos Aires we have our first day without fishing in weeks. I've never fished seventeen days in a row and likely never will again. This is nothing for a guide or some of my obsessed friends, but it's a lot for me.

After weeks in the country, being in a city feels strange. It's always hard to leave Patagonia. You miss people back home but you still don't want to leave. That's the rub, of course. Through our friends at Trevelin, we manage to get a good table and have a triumphant dinner at Don Julio, the *parrilla* where people wait hours to get in. Our waiter tells us we're sitting at table number 10, the best table, since that was Maradona's number. I'm not sure I believe that. Sounds like a fish story. But it's nice to be surrounded by people in the city.

Markley heads to Colombia, the next leg of his trip. He asks me to bring back rocks he's been collecting. So much for his light packing.

I move into the studio at the Jardin Escondido, I've got a few more days before I head home. I visit the gaucho tailor and sit in cafés. Buenos Aires is a good city to be in when you don't have a lot to do. I remember a story a guide told me about a young boy on a fishing trip with his father. He caught his first big trout, then took a moment to collect himself. He exhaled and said earnestly, *I did what I came here to do.* I hear you, kid.

In the cool evening I walk down the streets of Palermo. I think about the fishing and about my time down south. New York feels far away. But even after a day, Patagonia does too.

CHAPTER II

CUBA

An Overdue Engagement

In my early twenties, at an age when everything seems possible, I wrote down the countries I wanted to visit. Cuba was on top of that list. I thought it was only a matter of time before I would check into the Ambos Mundos and cultivate a vague air of mystery behind a cloud of cigar smoke. Plans and other priorities got in the way, as they do, and I never had the courage to enter illegally from Mexico. Over time, a trip that once felt inevitable looked like it would never happen.

Cuba remained in my imagination. I was entranced by the architecture, the music, and the baseball players who arrive in New York, their real ages unknown. Not to mention two of the twentieth century's most famous beards, worn by Cuban residents, Ernest Hemingway and Fidel Castro.

All of this was more illicit because Americans were forbidden to cross the ninety miles of water to visit the island. That's why Cuba feels farther away than it is. The world is much smaller than it was sixty years ago. But Cuba, for many of us, remained locked away. In the 1950s you could take your car on a ferry from Miami to Havana. Civilized. Now Americans go through extra paperwork and have to plan carefully. After more than two weeks in Cuba I'm still not sure if it was legal for me to be there.

When I told friends about my trip they asked if there are flights from the US to Cuba. There are. Every day, in fact. They look like every other flight, HAVANA illuminated in digital letters next to the gate. This is so easy it makes me nervous. I keep thinking something's going to happen, that somebody's going to say I don't have the right form and send me away, like at the DMV. Until I'm safely outside the Havana airport I don't believe I'll ever make it to Cuba.

My friend Matt and I arrive at the boarding gate and the scene is festive. People carry large shopping bags and taped-up boxes back with them, on the near side of legality, and look like they're moving out of a college dorm. They bring food and clothes and who knows what else back to friends and relatives in Havana. "There are more fake Rolexes here than I've ever seen in my life," Matt notes drily. I try to recall Marx's thoughts on the matter.

There's another reason to visit Cuba: the fishing. Not the marlin in the Gulf Stream of *The Old Man and the Sea*. But bonefish in the flats on the south side of the island. Tarpon in the rivers. And, don't hold your breath, the chance at a permit, the most difficult fish to catch that also happens to have the most mundane name. Add cigars, some old rum, and, as long as we're not detained and can avoid an international incident, everything's aligned for a good trip. That's not all. When the fishing is over we'll drive from Havana up the hill to the Finca Vigía and visit the house where Ernest Hemingway lived.

It's good to have a man in Havana, even though that means too many Graham Greene references. Ruaridh would not make an ideal spy. A tall, thin Scotsman with old-world charm and striking white hair—he's hard to forget. Ruaridh's name, which took some time for me to spell correctly, is pronounced *Rury* and is apparently common in Scotland. At least that's what he says. Ruaridh has lived in Havana for three years and his Spanish is enthusiastic and recalls Strunk's line that if you don't know how to pronounce a word say it loud. Ruaridh's love of the country is real though he's still pale as the Cliffs of Dover.

Ruaridh's traveled widely as a writer and editor for English newspapers and magazines. He was the DC correspondent for *The Observer* and reported from war zones in the Congo. Like many Scots, Ruaridh is, above all, an Atlantic salmon angler. Every year he makes his way to an enviable combination of rivers in Scotland, Iceland, and Canada to pursue the fish of a thousand casts. These trips are factored into his year and considered requisite, like visiting family. His success gives him a sense of assurance that I, who have not caught an Atlantic salmon, lack. Until I do, the Atlantic salmon remains the fish of ∞ casts.

Since Ruaridh has moved to Havana he's followed the vital maxim *fish where you live* and has made room in his heart for a saltwater practice he's taken up with fervor. Ruaridh has kindly helped with our arrangements: recommending drivers, booking fishing guides, reserving hotels, changing dollars to pesos at a favorable rate, and acquiring cigars. He also got us a local phone—what can you say about a friend like that?

Maybe he *is* a spy.

Matt and I land after the short flight from Miami and go through customs: Easy. We head out to meet Gustavo, who drives a vivid navy 1950s Cadillac. The sun is shining in Havana. Never in doubt.

We check in to the Jesús Maria, a small hotel in a restored family home, right off the harbor. The rooms are set around a courtyard and have tall ceilings and pale tile floors. I can see the water from my high window. Everything feels correctly proportioned—it's amazing how relaxed a fifteen-foot ceiling can make you. But maybe that's just the pleasure of arrival.

We sit at a small bar on the roof and look out toward the Gulf Stream. Ruaridh arrives with a smile and boxes of cigars. There's some discussion about whether the cigars are actually the Partagas and Hoyo de Monterreys the labels claim they are. "What I do know is that they're Cuban," he assures us. You can't argue with that.

Ruaridh is a new father. The presence of Ruaridh's son, Santiago, means that he will not be able to fish with us on our first stop. He's philosophical about his predicament (though he uses other language). Matt is in a more advanced state of fatherhood as his daughter has just left home for university at Edinburgh. Matt misses her, though he has more time to travel, to fish, and now has a good reason to visit Scotland.

I'm curious about the adjustment when anglers become fathers. Of course we start with the basic questions: the name of the boy, is he healthy, does he sleep through the night, which parent does he resemble, is your sanity intact. Then, after a respectful pause, *Do you miss the fishing?* Of course not, he says. Though a while later he asks about your recent fishing trip. You detect a sense of wistfulness in his voice. I undersell it. "The bonefish were fine. Just like the next time, they'll still be there." It's not clear either of us believes this.

These are complicated equations. Fishing casually requires time. Fishing seriously requires more time. Of course, babies require the most time. Fishing exists in friction with the other side of your life, the more responsible side. The push and pull between duties and escape is felt by anybody who travels to fish. After dinner at the theatrical La Guarida with its dramatic rooms and walls of peeling paint, Matt and I walk on the harbor and Ruaridh heads home.

Whatever the romance or illusions, Cuba is different on the other side. Everything is indirect, vague, or complicated. Americans convert cash on the black market. We can't use credit cards or stay at official hotels, which are owned by the government, and off-limits. Our technologically easy life back home, no doubt too easy, does not translate to Cuba. Your phone is basically useless, probably a good thing. We're close enough to sail to Miami, but feel far from home.

Everybody has a source for acquisitions that flirt with the wrong side of the law. Someone for butter. Another for olive oil (people at the Italian embassy are popular). A third for beef (Cuban cows belong to the government and are protected). Don't ask too many questions and you can probably get what you want, but it's a seller's market. People smuggle large coolers on boats from Florida and pray they aren't stopped by the coast guard. Before heading down, I asked Ruaridh for his wish list, which was good chocolate, a baby hat for Santiago, suntan lotion for the guides and coffee (his review: *the coffee here is shit*).

We have one day in Havana before heading to the water. Matt and I walk through the old town and pass the Floridita bar, which Ruaridh warns is a depressing set piece. Through the window we see a life-size statue of Hemingway, suffer a bad theme–park feeling, and keep moving.

We find our way to the Hotel Nacional. This institution has hosted, in former days of glory, everybody from Winston Churchill to Ava Gardner. We enter the white building, which looks like a day-old wedding cake, and pass through the immense lobby onto the lawn. Everything looks extravagant but underfunded. Along the wall are rows of bracingly unflattering photos of every notable guest who's ever visited. As if the hotel wants to make clear that Yes, we hosted these famous people but we don't care *too* much.

The Nacional is ideally situated on a hill above the harbor with views onto the water. People sit under arcades beside the lawn and drink daiquiris while peacocks ease by. A band of older men moves from table to table and plays surprisingly earnest ballads. I'm looking forward to my first Havana daiquiri. Fredo of course had his sad banana daiquiri in *The Godfather Part II* sitting in a square not far from here. Somehow we end up with frozen daiquiris, which look like they're from the children's menu. "This is the original way they were made," Matt says. "It's the coldest version there is." He notices my skepticism. "Do you know why?" I don't. "Because it was always hot as balls."

• • •

I look forward to fishing with Matt. I told him about this trip and hoped he would come. His enthusiasm didn't settle matters, however. His wife, a great friend, reminded me, *Matt says yes to everything.* Matt's *yes* was not enough. Every fishing trip runs through the angler's loved one. So I wrote his wife directly with the dates and asked if Matt's schedule had room for fishing. She keeps the master calendar, a powerful document, and proclaimed, *Matt can go,* but warned, *He has to be back in time for our trip to Rome.*

The opportunistic angler plans his year around the movements of the fish he loves. This is a combination of tides, migrations, and the hatches of insects. He blocks days off on his calendar. He books flights. He prays for an invitation to a private club. He hopes to graduate from the waiting list of his favorite Norwegian lodge. He's like those sharks that swim halfway around the world in anticipation of the poor seals that cross a channel one week a year.

Yes, that's the best way. But it's not the way for most of us, because a loved one will point out that she doesn't care one way or the other about the mayfly hatch in England and that you're expected to attend her cousin's wedding in the nice part of New Jersey. Don't you remember she mentioned this before? It does sound vaguely familiar. You pause, and ask innocently, *How close are you with this cousin?*

There are trade-offs. Live on the river or fish when your schedule allows. Even that can strain the bonds of love. Sometimes the issue is the symbolism of a fishing trip, which implies that angling is the real priority. *You plan these trips so long in advance. You and your friends. You and your fish.* I protest, *They aren't my fish, I wish they were my fish!*

Matt treads this line well. When he was a full-time photographer, he would include a day to scout locations. And this scouting was done with a fishing rod. I've learned from Matt that you have to be opportunistic—be happy when you can get on the water and strike when you have the chance.

Matt fishes the way he does everything: avidly, skillfully, with a priority on results, preferably immediate results. Patience is not Matt's preferred mode; it's not his unpreferred mode either. He will not be going on an Atlantic salmon trip with Ruaridh. Matt wants action and isn't fussy. He's brought a spinning rod and an ancient wooden plug in case he comes across a barracuda. There's something to be said for this direct approach and something, among fly fishing purists, to be said against it. *Purist* may be another word for *snob* and Matt will take action over snobbery any day.

Matt is descended from Italians and aspires to what he calls a Sicilian tan, the sight of which would send a dermatologist to a cardiologist. He encourages this by wearing jean cut-offs and no shirt while fishing for hours in direct sun. He'll hand me a bottle of suntan lotion, turn around, and say, *Time to do my back.* Conversely, my fair skin is aggressively covered in clothing and layers of SPF 1000. After the trip Matt looks like George Hamilton and I look like the Ghost of Christmas Past.

It's still dark out when we meet our driver. We wind our way out of the city as the sun comes up past men on the harbor wall casting into the sea. There are always people fishing in Havana. This direct declaration of optimism is a pure expression of the sport. Fly anglers, by contrast, are experts at indirectness always making things more complicated.

On Cuban highways anything is possible. Speeds range from 60 mph down to around 6 mph. Drivers must navigate around horse-drawn carts, old Chevys, motorcycles with sidecars, the occasional untrustworthy-looking bus. Everything is a different size, from a different decade, traveling at a different speed. There are Soviet-era cars I've never seen before. Matt knows them all. He recalls their vintages, failed marketing strategies, and exact resale value in Miami. *If we could get that Lada back to the States it's worth a lot.*

Ruaridh advises against driving at night. There are no lights. Pavement turns to dirt then back again. There are potholes so deep they have potholes inside them. Cars are expensive and hitchhiking is part of life. People line up at the highway entrance waving bills they'll pay to anybody who picks them up.

After an hour of careful navigation we pull onto a dirt road. Children wearing khaki uniforms head to school, riding on bike handlebars or walking with their mothers. Chickens wander the yards of spare buildings. We keep turning down roads that get narrower and rougher. The air is humid. Every angler feels a thrill seeing new water for the first time. I get more excited the longer we have to wait. The mystery builds.

Finally, we pull up to a gate, the entrance to a national preserve. Tire tracks run through tall, patchy grass leading to a dock and a low, flat motorboat. Two large tables sit under a pavilion. Matt and I prepare our rods, reels, and flies. The fly boxes are still perfectly arranged, our plans are still intact.

We meet Felipe, who's relaxed, friendly, and has the enthusiasm of a youth soccer coach. He's also one of the most celebrated guides in Cuba. By now, Matt and I have turned the tables into a complete inventory of our gear. Felipe takes a closer look at our flies—by tradition we bring too many—and points out some of his favorites. Matt's theory, really more of a life approach, is that he never wants to be, in his words, *under-geared*. Master of the double-duffel-bag-pack, he's never been under-geared in his life. We load everything into the boat, which is covered in a vinyl carpet last seen in a suburban basement in the 1980s. Aside from the carpet, this reminds me of the johnboats I fish from in Wisconsin rivers for smallmouth bass. But we're not fishing for bass; we're fishing for tarpon.

The tarpon is an ancient fish, prehistoric in appearance, with a jutting jaw, fierce eyes, and silver scales the size of a fist. The tarpon grows well over a hundred pounds and is bigger than your nephew. These fish take over people's lives—they become addicted to fighting them on light tackle. We've got a more modest agenda, pursuing baby tarpon, ten to twenty-five pounds. Don't be fooled. Nothing feels small about a baby tarpon caught on a fly rod.

Baby tarpon are Matt's favorite fish. Tarpon take a fly in a dramatic darting swoosh and, moments later, jump clear of the water, then slam down again in a tremendous crash. Tarpon fishing is theatrical, highly visual, and fighting one is real work.

Tarpon need to be seen moving. They're not themselves when still. They swim slowly, at a regal pace, then incredibly fast when chasing food—a blaze of reflected light in the water. They burst to life when hooked, they jump and twist and writhe. This performance—many feet out of the water—staggers anybody lucky enough to witness it. The shock of seeing an immense fish at our eye level deafens us to everything else in the world. The fish shakes its massive body, and we hear the whirring sound, like a boomerang, water thrown in every direction, before it falls back into the ocean. Then there's just the voice of your friend: *Whoa.* That's tarpon fishing, buddy, and, like backcountry skiing or high-stakes poker, you realize why the adrenaline surge invites addiction.

Now it's our turn to see who becomes addicted to what. Felipe eases the boat into the channel, and we speed past mangroves, herons blending into the branches as they hunt slowly along the shore. The channel widens until we are about to enter wider water when Felipe cuts the engine. At first I'm worried something is wrong with the boat. But tarpon often arrive here in the morning, Felipe says. I tie on a Purple Bunny—a bad name for a good fly—large and furry, with a thin tail that resembles a darting minnow when stripped quickly. Tarpon chase baitfish and we want to imitate that speed.

In the distance we can make out patterns of disturbance, like raindrops marking the surface of the river: A school of tarpon. The tarpon break through the water and into our sight to gulp for air with their enormous mouths. They also do this to feed. Cast in front of them and hopefully one crashes your minnow. "Sometimes they come to the surface, sometimes they stay down." Felipe pauses. "Tarpon is complicated."

I've never caught a tarpon of any size. I try to be ready for their persistence; like striped bass, they'll keep coming for the fly even if they've missed it. Sometimes I'll stop stripping—the fish is just so close to the boat!—and I want to give it a last chance to take the fly. But then they lose interest and disappear.

"Oh!" Felipe exclaims. "They're already here." Matt doesn't waste time. He has his fly in the water. The school we saw disappeared—they change directions a lot—but they're quickly back. Before I even stand up, Matt is fighting a fish that makes the famous tarpon leap close to the boat, and soon the fish is at hand. A dream start for Matt.

Guides like it when their sports catch fish within the first five minutes—who wouldn't? Felipe laughs and navigates into the wide river and sets the anchor. In the distance we hear the water breaking and see ripples in the surface. "Get ready," Felipe says. I cast in their direction. Suddenly the surface is quiet. "They're down deep,"

Felipe reassures us. I cast a few more times, and as I strip in a bright streak blazes toward my fly at astonishing speed. It misses. I'm in shock and stop stripping. "Don't stop!" Felipe says. Don't worry about a miss, give the fish a second chance.

The school is downriver, but they circle back toward the boat. I cast and try to intersect their path. This is not trout fishing where you want a nice drift along the current. Here you're imitating a fleeing baitfish, and you haul the fly in by quickly stripping the line toward you. Nothing happens. More stripping. More nothing. Then a flash. Almost bronze under the water, like something from antiquity. I was expecting this—or hoping for it anyway—and yet the violence is a complete shock. I keep stripping and the tarpon comes back from the other direction. This time I feel the fish. I set, set again, and the tarpon is on. "*Yes!*" Matt exclaims, laughing.

I'm reeling with no strategy to speak of. This is a strong, fighting fish. I reel as fast as I can until there's resistance, a full stop. I wait then reel more slowly. I can't tell where the fish is, when suddenly the tarpon is in the air right in front of us, parallel to the water. I lean forward and point my rod down toward the water, as I've been told to do, so the line doesn't break. My first tarpon! My first tarpon jump! Now I'm enjoying the moment. The tarpon jumps again, and shakes in the air. I lean forward again. After the tarpon lands, the Purple Bunny floats lazily in the air. The fly and the fish are traveling in opposite directions, never a good situation. This is no longer my first tarpon! I am no longer enjoying the moment!

Felipe laughs in a friendly way. "That happens," he says. "You don't land every tarpon." We'll have more chances. Later I note that Felipe didn't give me much guidance during the fight. Matt says, "He thought it looked like you knew what you were doing." I parse this sentence with a profound sense of ambivalence.

Ancient animals are the simplest, most elemental. They are evolutionary expressions of their purpose. A tarpon is all scales. Of course all fish are scales. But these scales are not seamless and invisible, they interlock like a silver chessboard, like armor.

Anglers who fight huge tarpon make them change directions. The fish has to be disoriented and not allowed to dictate the situation. Tarpon anglers fight immense fish for over an hour. But the best anglers manage to land them more quickly. Once a tarpon takes control it fights harder, you're reacting to what it wants to do and you're at a major disadvantage. I learn this firsthand later when suddenly I'm hooked up to another one.

My fight takes too long. I'm too reactive, Felipe tells me later. This tarpon is deep and I work hard to bring it up. Depending on your point of view, five minutes is about the right amount of time to reel in a fish you can't see. The fish tires. After ten minutes, I'm tired too. I can't imagine fighting one of these fish for an hour and then losing it.

In most saltwater fishing there are no nets. The fish comes to rest alongside the boat and the guide (if you're with one) reaches down and takes it by the mouth. Unhooking a Purple Bunny from a tarpon is more involved than freeing a Parachute Adams from a trout. Felipe leans in and opens its enormous mouth, pulls the hook out, and lets the fish swim next to the boat while it recovers. The silver tarpon looks like the oldest creature I've ever seen. Fifteen pounds, Felipe says. Though probably smaller. I don't mind. I'm just happy to be in the game.

"That's good," Matt says. The boat succeeds together. But the boat really succeeds when Matt catches the first tarpon.

Lunch in Cuba is not like lunch in Argentina. Felipe's brought some sardines he's acquired through an unnamed source. We have them with brown bread and I drink a beer I've never seen before and don't need to see again. I've always thought that bad beer remains better than no beer. This really challenges that premise.

We head down another channel, beneath an archway of mangroves. This narrows into a dramatic corridor of branches that feels like we're in *Apocalypse Now*. Away from the breeze on the open river the air is still and we feel the humidity. Felipe poles the boat to an opening where there's enough room to cast. We're in close quarters. Short casts to fish twenty feet away. Then the challenge begins— we can't let the tarpon enter the mangroves or they'll break off.

"I hear them," Felipe says. And there's the school, crashing through the water, farther up the corridor. It's like a horror film where you hear the monster coming before you can see it. I cast ahead and start stripping. They're on top of us and I'm connected to a fish. It heads to the man-

grove, just a few feet away, and suddenly I'm not connected to the fish anymore. The fish, my fly, the leader,
everything, is gone. Again Felipe's nonjudgmental laugh.
But this is exciting. Matt has better luck, gets one on the
line and refuses to let the fish make it into the mangroves.
Of course you can break off a tarpon, the fly snapping, by
not letting it run. But he brings a fish in quickly. Impressive. In the shade, the tarpon looks even more mysterious. Their black backs, the deep silver, a barely controlled
strength waiting to explode.

It's my turn again. The action is fast. The tarpon have
headed down the channel but Felipe says they'll be back.
"They have nowhere else to go." Back they come, echoing
through this hallway of wood and water.

Mangroves are peaceful but if the tarpon enters that
underwater thicket, then that's that. But landing a large
fish on light tackle isn't easy. This is why you want to
fight a fish in open water where it can run. That's not the
equation here. They head to the mangroves and you can't
let them.

I hook up with one so close to the boat I'm staggered.
Most fish don't like the sight of boats—they have to be
distracted by their prey. I keep the pressure on and manage to corral it to Felipe, who's waiting at the side of the
boat. Smaller than the first fish. Nobody cares. We have
some bad beer and head back to the river. We're done for
the day.

Ruaridh is waiting for us at the takeout. He's happy
everything went well but wishes he could have fished too.
We are driving down to Playa Larga, a beach town. We

thank Felipe and look forward to seeing him the next day. We're heading to the flats.

It's easy to forget that the Bay of Pigs, like Watergate, was a place before it became a historical event. The Watergate always strikes me as a nondescript building that caused such a scandal. The Bay of Pigs, likewise, is attractive but would not stand out among other seaside towns. The only difference is that entering the marina we are greeted with a tank pointing toward the water, as if the island is on a military footing, quite precarious, it must be said. Like other military displays around Cuba it has the effect of an oversize model that looks more like a toy than the first line of defense.

The town is a loose gathering of buildings, empty lots, and low-lying houses along a beach. Of the many boats roped to the docks, few look seaworthy. Freestanding stalls dot a parking lot, like small bodegas, where a person sits selling cigarettes, candy, and crucially, aged Cuban rum which we cannot get back in New York. Aged rum is brown, not too sweet, needs nothing but ice, though lime if you like, and is superb. It's like warm weather Scotch. This is the best thing you can drink in the country by a wide margin. Ruaridh's favorite is Santiago 11-Year, which we enjoyed in Havana. That's hard to find. Here we order Havana Club 7-Year. Which is also excellent. Matt takes a sip and then another. He reflects for a moment and points at the glass. "That is a damn fine beverage."

We're staying at a modest guesthouse right on the beach.

Hanging over my bed is an image of a bass fishing boat with a red neon border, which may have once been in a Knoxville barbecue joint. Outside is a narrow bar and a few tables under a terrace. A woman sits in the shade and keeps track of everybody's tab in a notebook. She manages the employees and, to a lesser extent, her guests. The bar serves eggs in the morning, some local melon, and coffee so strong it barely moves.

She asks what we want for dinner, which, as we sit and watch the sun come up over the ocean, seems a long way off. Ruaridh tells her if the cook can get a snapper we'd love that. There may be an irony that we're going fishing but the fish we catch won't be coming back with us. Many fly anglers, by rule or preference, are catch and release practitioners, and have gotten over that irony long ago.

For fifty years these flats were protected and rarely fished. Castro didn't allow development and they remained an oasis that could only be dreamed about. That changed two decades ago, and outfitters began bringing anglers to Cuba, though the number fluctuates depending on the political situation. The conditions are good. We have no excuses.

At the edge of town is a gate to the national preserve. A man, who still harbors Communist sympathies, wears shorts over longer shorts, has a large white mustache and a distrust of *los Yanquis*. No small talk, no smile, no fake Rolex. He warily inspects the Jeep and our licenses, as it turns out he does every day of our trip, even though we're in one of the only cars to pass through the gate.

Ruaridh drives us down a dirt road lined with trees that become farther and farther apart. Between them we see immense flats of water with hundreds of birds—flamingos, ibises, swifts. This is a gathering place on their migratory path and they're everywhere. Flamingos seem to walk on the water with their long legs, like chopsticks, as they pick up enough speed to take off. It's joyous entering this kingdom of water and sunlight, sand and birds.

At the end of the road is a dock where guides stand talking to each other in loud, rapid Spanish beside narrow flatboats, designed for one captain and one angler. You don't see your friends until the end of the fishing day. Then you ask with mixed emotions how they did. You want them to do well, naturally, but if you struggled you don't want to hear that they had the day of days, at least not until you've recovered with your rum.

This is our routine and it's a good one. We rotate guides, and after a few days I head out with Juan Carlo, who's compact, highly strung, and speaks excellent English. Apparently, he studies the dictionary every morning in the john. I sense that Juan Carlo misses his previous sport, Matt. "Matteo," he says longingly, "Matteo loved to fish for barracuda." He makes it sound as if Matteo is ailing somewhere. Unlike Matteo I don't bring a special rod with a wire leader to fish for barracuda. I'm here for bonefish.

Juan Carlo, even when pining for Matteo, puts you on bonefish. A good guide takes into account the tides and the flats where bonefish arrive to feed. Also the passages between the flats where fish move as water levels change. Then there's the physical side: poling the boat and stopping it, all quietly so as not to disturb the fish. He does this with his head raised, eyes scanning endless stretches of water, looking for signs of life. He wants to put his angler in the right place so he can cast, ideally with the wind at his back toward an approaching bonefish. Guides also have to decide, in the absence of fish, how long to wait before leaving a flat. This means cutting your losses and heading another ten or twenty minutes away to a flat that everybody knows was not the first choice. That's all before dealing with demanding New Yorkers. It's a hard job.

As Juan Carlo gets more comfortable with me he gets more philosophical. "When you lose a bonefish it's lamentable but okay," he explains. "When you lose a permit it's just lamentable." This is a rare irrefutable fishing truth, right down to "lamentable." Here's other advice I heard during days on the flats in varying levels of translation, and mistranslations of fishing theories are better than proper translations:

Bonefish is a different school every day. Juan Carlo says this out of admiration and resignation. Observe, learn, and still we never understand them.

Bonefish is allowed to do what he wants to do. Accept bonefish and their idiosyncrasies instead of fuming. This is true in all fishing. And I like the idea though I don't always follow the principle.

Bonefish is a bastard. I have a lot of warm feelings toward the bonefish. But a bonefish that chases and then rejects a perfectly good fly definitely possesses capacities of bastard-dom, bastardocity, and severe bastardliness. In Cuba certainly, they have the objectionable quality of the *bastardo*.

Juan Carlo mentions the possibility of casting to a permit. *Casting to* a permit is different than *catching* a permit. Are you familiar with the permit? If you know what a permit is, then you've probably fished for them. That means you have a very happy or a very sad story to tell. There's no in-between with permit. Fly anglers are intent on trying to ruin their lives and nothing breaks the spirit like a permit. If you don't know what a permit is, don't go down this path of pain, doubt, and recrimination. Get out while you still can!

A permit is a wonderful and, to the uninitiated, an unusual-looking fish. Noble to the angler and, I'm sorry to say, somewhat curious, even silly, to newcomers. Flat is the first thing most people will notice: A permit is all surface, compressed silver. They're shy, strong, and comically difficult to catch. Naturally, that makes them appealing. Showing rare discipline I declare that I'm not going to hijack my time in Cuba chasing permit. But if we see the stack telltale forked tail then, naturally, I'll be happy to cast to one. Juan Carlo says this current gives us a good chance to see permit moving through certain flats. I enter that into the large volume of *Collected Statements of Overly Optimistic Guides*, and forget about it.

I have a 9wt rod tied with a crab pattern that, in the extremely rare chance we see a permit, will be suitable. I'm armed with this rod while staring at the water—there's nowhere else to stare, but I wouldn't say I'm focused on it. The intensity of my vision comes and goes. So I'm startled to hear Juan Carlo exclaim, *"There!"*

Forty feet away, instantly recognizable, is a permit's tail. Similar to the bonefish tail, but taller and slightly darker. The wind is at our backs, we're in a perfect position. I have enough time to make one false cast and then send the line out. Since I haven't been expecting this permit, I'm not a wreck of nervous anticipation. I consider a new approach to fishing and possibly my entire life: *Just relax and cast. Get out of your own head. Nice and easy, no stress, man.* If this works out I might move to L.A., grow weed, and wear a bathrobe in public.

I start my motion and let instinct take over. Instinct is going to make the perfect cast to this permit and instinct is going to catch it. Instinct cuts through the noise of over-analysis and doubt. Instinct understands what I've practiced for decades, grabs the wheel and takes control. I release my cast and send the crab toward the permit and it lands in the water. Everything is crystalized in this moment. I have a revelation, perfectly clear in the afternoon sunshine: Instinct has driven off a cliff.

The cast I made by instinct, one of the most significant of my life, did not interfere with the permit in any demonstrable way. Most charitably the cast could be said to be in the *general vicinity* of the permit, the same way that if a friend is across Grand Central Terminal you're in their general vicinity. But you don't expect to run into each other. And I don't run into the permit.

In a curious turn of events, the fact that the cast was so horrific actually gives me another chance. But now instinct is no longer in charge. Instinct had its chance and failed. Instinct took a potentially valuable life-altering moment and lit it on fire. Enough of instinct. Instinct is in the shredder. Now that I'm aware how badly I bungled this initial cast—the fish was in the perfect location and people go days without even seeing a permit—analysis and self-doubt have reentered the equation. And they're back with a vengeance.

The permit closes toward the boat, it's twenty feet away. Now I have to be very delicate here, very precise. Precision, however, is no longer in my mental or physical equation. My system, a moment ago sailing on a sea of tranquility, has been hijacked by a profound case of the wobbles, since we're in Cuba a case of *los wobblés*. My next cast is not on the nose of the permit. It's not on the tail either, not remotely. I overshoot the fish by ten feet, because I still have too much line out from the previous cast. The permit keeps swimming out of sight and out of my life. And suddenly the whole thing is over. It's gone.

Juan Carlo says nothing. What happened can't be laughed off. Many fish are lost in a complex intersection of human and animal, physics and technology. Not this time. There's no consolation for this nadir of amateurism, which has the irrefutable stench of scoring an own goal in soccer. Yes, Juan Carlo remains quiet, but we're both thinking the same thing.

Lamentable.

• • •

We return to the decidedly lower stakes world of the bonefish. Juan Carlo, I come to realize, is no romantic; he's a shark. He has high standards for himself and for whoever's in his boat. Juan Carlo wants me to do things I can't—or think I can't—do. In a perfect world I would meet the challenge and prove him right and myself wrong. In this world, however, I'm breaching my comfort zone. Does that mean I wisely know my limits? Or does it mean I cower away from a new level of respectability? I find myself blaming the person who expects great things from me but is simply clarifying my shortcomings.

Sometimes I have to tell Juan Carlo I need a moment to regroup, to change a deteriorating fly, or just to exhale. Or that I can't cast sixty feet into the wind over the back of a bonefish swimming away on the off, off, off chance he'll turn to take it. For him, every minute not fishing is a wasted minute. Every cast not taken is a wasted opportunity. After a few days with Juan Carlo my habits are leaner, more efficient. I land fish faster, release them more quickly, check the leader and the fly to make sure they're in good shape, then return to the platform ready to cast again. There's no break to celebrate. This isn't exactly leisurely, but we do well together. I'm operating on Juan Carlo's time. On the last day everything goes to plan. I've never caught so many bonefish.

In the hotel I'm asked to move into an even smaller room that's narrow, white, spartan, with vividly colored star stick-

ers arrayed across the ceiling, like a psychedelic constella-
tion. It feels like it belongs in a convent if the nuns loved
disco. There's a window with a grate with an obscured view
onto a cement walkway, a leaking air conditioner, a small
table, and a shower that decides what temperature the water
will be. This is a room I would only stay in if I'm fishing.

One morning I'm greeted by a gentle pale gray dog.
Many of the dogs on the streets are unusually distinguished.
This dog has white eyes, from glaucoma, that give an otherworldly quality to a sweet animal. A friendly ghost. When I
return at the end of the day, the dog is joined by a cat, also
with white eyes, like marbles. Eerie.

I think of a bonefish I saw earlier that didn't react to
my fly. Not curious, but not scared either. It swam steadily
right up to the boat. Soon a shark arrived and the bonefish
didn't flee. I had a bad feeling about the situation, but the
shark didn't react either. Maybe the bonefish couldn't see
or be seen. I like to think of this phantom bonefish, slowly
roaming the tidal flats, free to swim in peace.

Matt leaves for New York, tomorrow he'll be in Rome.
Ruaridh's back in Havana with his family. Ruaridh and
I were supposed to fish another place he intriguingly
described as *strange even for Cuba*, but he's recalled on
domestic duties. Our party has gone quiet and I'm alone.
I watch the sun come up every morning with a man who's
always on the beach smoking a cigar. After fishing I swim
in the ocean as the sun goes down. By the last night the
bottle of rum is empty. I have dinner and go to sleep early.

• • •

After the disco nunnery, La Reserva Hotel in Havana feels doubly luxurious. The neighborhood has lovely mansions in competing stages of disrepair. After fishing and the sun and the salt I try to prepare myself for seeing people again. Ruaridh, Camila, and Santiago pick me up to drive to the Finca Vigía. The old farm became Hemingway's home and he lived there for more than twenty years, when this was still a quiet area.

We pull past a lawn that has seen better days and park near a gift shop I'm afraid to enter. We buy tickets in a small room beneath a photo, often reproduced in Cuba, of Hemingway and Castro standing next to each other. At the top of the hill is the house essentially as Hemingway left it. After he died, the Kennedy administration, who'd invited Hemingway to JFK's inauguration (he declined), arranged to get his papers back, a delicate negotiation at that fraught time between the two countries. The deal suited both parties: The house would remain as it was and be open to the public.

Hemingway's house is a well-furnished, tiled villa with bookshelves, dark wood furniture he had made, and long views down across Havana to the sea. In the simplest terms, it's nice. Delightful even. Reassuringly solid, but airy and dignified. There's a large record player, a reproduction of a Joan Miró painting he bought from the artist in Spain, and enough mounted animal heads to start a natural history museum, taxidermy serving as his default décor.

This is a bright place to live well. Martha Gellhorn arranged for the farm to be restored, but Hemingway was skeptical it could be brought back to life. While he was away from the island she went ahead with the renovation. He came back and fell in love with the house and out of love with her. She said marrying him was the worst decision in her life and she meant it.

It's forbidden to enter the house—tall windows give onto every room and, like voyeurs, we stand outside and peer into the living quarters. We're the only visitors and walk slowly around the grounds. The pool, now empty, is big enough for a resort. This isn't a one-room cabin on a pond where you sharpen your pencils for exercise. This is a place you host Gary Cooper. The *Pilar*, Hemingway's fishing boat, sits on blocks in the shade under a corrugated metal roof where the tennis court used to be. The tower, where he would often write, is closed the day we are there, sealed with a thin thread attached to a wax seal that's used by the cultural ministry to keep people from crossing into places they aren't allowed to go.

We know the evidence of this life—the work, the letters, the photographs. Hemingway's was one of the most documented lives in the twentieth century. And yet I realize I never heard his voice until recently. It was higher than I expected. Biographies can leave an unsettled feeling. A complete life gets exhausting when we're confronted with stark details. How many animals shot, wives mistreated, children neglected, friends eviscerated. The myth is built, then the myth is dismantled. Hemingway's writing can be impossible to see away from that distraction. This house, however, is real. Where everything else is disputed, this is close to fact. The wall next to the scale in the bathroom is covered in small numbers written in pencil, Hemingway recording his weight every day. This is the most personal part of the house, private and human. The antidote to iconography.

We drive down toward Havana and have late lunch on the deck at Santi's looking onto the canal. We eat shrimp and grilled squid and talk about children and families. I thank Ruaridh for his hospitality. I'll miss him when I leave.

He drops me at the hotel as weather arrives. Rain in Havana is very convincing. The walls shake, the staff moves furniture around and hides things in closets. It's my last day here. After the rain I walk through the neighborhood and pass a man I've seen before. He smokes a cigarette and repairs his Russian car. We nod to each other.

Life in Cuba feels dictated by invisible powers and far-off battles. What happens when the legends have been told so many times nobody can remember if they're real anymore? I keep thinking about the tarpon in the mangroves. An ancient fish in an older part of the world, outside of time. You shouldn't be in a place that wild for long, you don't belong there. Dark clouds build up in the harbor and I walk back to the hotel just before the rain returns.

CHAPTER III

BELIZE

A Reckless Ambition

Hanging on the wall of our cabin in Wisconsin is a framed illustration the size of a placemat—maybe it *was* a placemat from a nearby lodge, long closed—with drawings of the biggest fish caught in the area. All the local characters are there: the fearsome northern pike, the uncomplicated largemouth bass, the genial bluegill. Curiously, the fish are not portrayed to scale, so they all look roughly the same size. Together, they resemble a mismatched family portrait.

Beneath each fish is a list of the exact dimensions, the name of the triumphant angler, the body of water where the feat took place, and the day it was caught, all in the decade after World War II. These are the records I like—regional, obsolete, not photographed. We use our imaginations, which gives the exercise the power of a children's story or something repeated by a grandfather so often that it starts to feel true.

I try not to get caught up in the benchmarks of the sport. You don't want to get too clinical about the whole enterprise. There's something to be said for the ten-pound bonefish, whose girth is more expansive than its streamlined colleagues that I catch. I can't imagine landing a thirty-pound salmon. Once you start chasing trophies your perspective starts to change. That's why some anglers have foresworn the pleasures of the trout and even the salmon, the foundational fish of our sport. Instead, they're fixated on the hundred-pound tarpon, the only fish that keeps their attention. Good for them.

There's another rare accomplishment, however, that's more elastic: the grand slam. The grand slam requires catching three saltwater fish—the bonefish, the tarpon, and the mercurial permit—on the same day. They can be any size, but they must be caught from sunup to sundown. Whoever invented this no doubt accomplished the feat and decided to name it. Now enterprising lodge owners promise over-eager sports a chance at angling immortality.

I politely dismiss the grand slam and gently shake my

head at the desperate grasping of these, these . . . *status-seekers*. The emptiness in their souls can only be filled with symbols of their own accomplishment. Thankfully I'm not susceptible to the worship of false idols. I seek a more modest angling connection free of vainglory. Fishing success happens privately and there's no number for that—there can't be—it's too personal.

That's what I tell myself, anyway. I'm like the man who shuns the club out of principle, but the principle might be that he's afraid he can't get in. Over time the grand slam has attracted my attention in a vague way, like a flicker of light on the horizon while driving through the desert. As I drive closer, the light grows brighter and I want to see its source. This is because of the sheer improbability of the endeavor. I'm not that greedy, I don't need the grand slam, and don't want it. I'd be happy to catch a permit. Wanting to catch a permit, however, is very greedy indeed.

No, I don't need to catch a permit. I just want a *good shot* at catching a permit. This language is nuanced, almost lawyerly. Once you admit you want a shot at a permit, it's all over, the angling gods have you. You think you can stay on the outside but who are you kidding? It's never enough. You want a chance at a permit? It's already too late. Once a permit is on the list you're going to get hurt.

The founding flaw in the angler's logic is the premise that you *just want to see the fish*. Anglers say many things that are half true. The least half true is the innocent declaration that we'd be happy just seeing a fish. This is the equivalent of the team that's just happy to be in the big game. Nonsense. From there it escalates.

These crucial steps explain the angler's psychology that inevitably lead to heartbreak. When there are no signs of life our sport can feel demoralizing. We've been on the water, nothing is happening and, after a few hours, we say, quite rightly, that we *just want to see a fish*. That's all. Just see a permit. One will do. Look, there it is. But here I am. And in my hand is a rod and reel, procured at great expense, anticipating this moment.

So, naturally enough, I *just want to cast to the fish*. I want to give myself a chance after all. Who wouldn't want a sense of sport? I mean, how do you test yourself against the great challenge of catching a permit unless you cast? Yes, one cast. One cast and one chance. This is my moment. How nice. But not really that nice.

Because now you *just want the fish on the line*. Nothing more really, a simple connection. You want to convince the wary permit to take the crab pattern that you cast in front of it. The take is everything. Landing a fish is anticlimactic. Just a connection and I'll be happy. Sure, sure. I'd like to believe you, I really would.

That state of affairs is quickly over because now you *just want to fight the fish*. Who wouldn't? It's a permit. A fish of legendary strength that will go on a searing run, peeling off line. A singular thrill. You want to be joined to a fish that's so alive the energy travels up the rod and puts a charge into your arm. You just want to feel the permit on the line, is that too much to ask? Well, yes.

Because once it's on the line you *just want to bring the permit close to the boat*. And if you've got the fish, especially a permit, all the way to the boat, then my goodness you want to land that fish. I mean do you have any emotions at all? Are you human? Do you live and breathe and have a sense of wonder about your place in the world? Have you ever, in a private moment, considered the possibility of a higher power? Good grief, of course you want to catch that permit! What's the point of being alive if you don't want to catch a permit? *It's a permit!*

Well, I'm glad we settled that. As you can see, we're a long way from wanting to see the permit and closer to why we will always continue to fish. We try to convince ourselves we want something modest. But it's not modest and never was. We start small but then we want it all. You don't have to come out and say that, but it probably helps.

These theoretical considerations come into focus as I fly down to Placencia, the southernmost city in Belize. This is where I can see a permit, and maybe catch one. I just want a chance. Though the difference between seeing a permit and catching one, as I know perfectly well, is the difference between four cards and a royal flush. You're going to need to draw that ace. And it has to be the right suit.

The permit remains vague to most of society. A permit is not a sight people come across in their everyday lives. They're not in a fish market or on a menu. You can't find one even if you try. Anglers hear about permit long before they see them. They read stories that feel as far off as long ago wars, the glory set in time. The name is unusually clinical for an animal. Especially one as strong and fast as a permit. The permit was clearly not named by a poet. This is not a functionary or bureaucrat; it's a bold streak of silver.

If you decide to get to the bottom of things and look up a permit, you might be surprised what causes this uninhibited desire. An Atlantic salmon impresses all who survey it. A brown trout is a fish without flaw. The reverence for permit is not in concert with its appearance. Beneath "PERMIT" you will find a photo of an unobtrusive, sail-shaped fish. You might be taken by the flatness of the permit and it's undignified to compare it to a pancake. But narrowness is one of the permit's distinguishing features.

Yes, the permit is improbable. One large eye stares out from its side, like a black gumdrop. The silver turns darker closer to the back and culminates in the prominent forked gray tail, the source of the permit's incredible speed. In a certain light there seems a faint reflection of yellow below its gills. This is definitely a saltwater fish— a version of what you would find swimming innocuously in an aquarium.

Anglers make decisions they come to regret. One of the worst decisions is getting mixed up with permit. Why do we do these things? Why? We don't eat permit. We don't mount them over the desks of our studies (or shouldn't anyway). Some anglers in the 1970s began fishing for tarpon and bonefish on light tackle. They rarely, oh so rarely, started to see permit. And well, they thought, why don't we give it a shot?

The permit was diabolically hard to catch, which naturally didn't deter them. They became addicted to those miraculous occasions when they *did* get a permit on the line, and the fish would make impossible runs. This was noted by the aficionados and dead-enders in the greater Key West area who were fishing when they weren't dabbling in saltwater poetry. Who wouldn't trust the collective wisdom of a group dedicated to beer, rum, and Bolivian marching powder? Word spread, and so did the locations where anglers realized permit could be found.

Farther south in Cuba, in the Bahamas, and in Belize, among other places. People who should have been happy pursuing bonefish or a few immense tarpon now swore off those pleasures for a fish they had far, far less chance of catching. You just can't navigate what makes sense when you're on the water. There's a chance, however remote, of catching a permit. *We're already here*, one angler says to another, sealing their fate. *The permit should come onto the flat with the afternoon tide. Let's try it. What harm could come of it?*

What harm indeed.

My permit experience has been a litany of nerves and bad casting. I've dipped my toe in some undignified waters. The last lamentable permit I saw was back in Cuba. I failed in mundane rather than spectacular fashion. Fishing for permit is a punctuation of action followed by a piercing disappointment. Permit fishing does not involve gentle rhythms, a smooth process, or even relaxation. Yes, you are in a beautiful place doing something you love, but disaster is stalking you at every waking moment. Like people who rode in hot air balloons a hundred years ago—the view's beautiful but the whole thing could erupt in flames at any moment. Your love constantly threatens to sour.

The problems *really* start when you see the permit. Now you are in the arena. Now there are stakes. A moment ago you were staring off the bow philosophically contemplating the nature of desire. Well what you wanted just showed up. Be careful what you wish for. Don't forget to breathe.

The first permit I saw was a number of years ago in Belize with Matt. Our trip had been delayed by snow along the East Coast. We made it down a day late but conditions weren't great. The weather was gray and cold and the bonefish were hard to catch. We waded on a famous flat beneath a low bank of clouds. Suddenly we came upon two tailing permit. Our whole trip had a chance to be redeemed. After ten mediocre casts I made a few that were right on their nose.

The permit didn't respond. There wasn't a huge blowup. They didn't spook. They just didn't care. "The crab was where it should be," I insisted, ignoring the flailing efforts and focusing on more limited samples of my best work. Matt had a different interpretation of the events. He was sure the permit had veered toward my side of the flat— we were fifty feet apart, with Martin, our wonderful guide, between us. Matt's efforts had been similarly rebuffed, but he fixated on the fact that he, in his assessment, had fewer chances than I did. Martin smiled, "It's permit, man."

I returned to Belize more recently. I wasn't expecting permit success but was open to the possibility. My first morning, I arrived at the boat with the requisite combination of excitement and anxiety. "What do you want to do, catch a permit?" the guide, Charlie, asked with what I detected was a sense of dismissiveness. Was this a trick question? "Well I'd like to see a permit, who wouldn't?" I thought this was a safe response.

"Well, we can go if you want to," Charlie said, without enthusiasm. "But it's a forty-five-minute ride in the waves. It's windy and the fish might not even come up. It's your call." I didn't have a lot of room to maneuver. I, a permit novice—what's the step below novice?—was in no position to overrule the guru. We agreed to try tomorrow.

I returned to the hotel with a profound sense of anticlimax. I tried to read a book, but no spy thriller could live up to chasing a permit. The next day I showed up at the pier and Charlie wasn't there. I waited then went back to the hotel. Somebody at the desk called him. Apparently he was at home, figuring I wouldn't want to head out, as the fishing looked bad again. Perhaps he imagined, was certain in fact, that I would agree with him.

On the third day, not sure what to expect, I showed up at the dock, and there was Charlie. We took the panga, the large open boat common in Belize, down the canal behind the hotel and out away from Placencia and into open water. We passed the small islands lining the Belize coast. Some are hotels with a dock and a handful of brightly painted buildings. Others are uninhabited, surrounded by reefs. Finally we arrived at a flat that ran between two deep sections of the ocean. When the tide changed, the permit would come up into the shallows to feed on crabs. That was the theory, anyway.

We got out of the boat and waded in steep waves. I had been hoping, foolishly, to be casting to a permit on a tranquil flat. No such luck. The wind was up, the sky was bruised, the water off-color. Prospects were dim. Morale wasn't too hot either.

I just want to see a permit! Is that too much to ask? That question, as we know, is the first step down a slippery slope. I was embarrassed the thought ever entered my mind. The whole endeavor felt absurd. I was standing in the water dutifully holding my rod and fly, with fifty or sixty feet of fly line trailing behind me. I was trying to stay in the game.

In a river the banks form a contour of possibility that brings a certain logic to the process. There are only so many places the fish can be. Like guessing a number between one and ten. In an ocean the odds feel oppressive. The permit can be anywhere, a number between one and a thousand. Nothing suggested this was anything less than idiotic, vanity expressing itself far from shore.

"There!" Charlie yelled. Miracle of miracles, the dark tail of the permit rose out of the water. Game on. In the waves it was hard to see, but there could be no mistake. The hotel had sent a photographer with us (a long story), and Charlie, in advanced years, brought an assistant, who pulled the boat behind us while we waded. That meant I was attempting to pull off one of the most difficult feats in the sport while being photographed in front of a small audience. All things considered—a gray day, wind, waves—I

was well positioned to cast. Charlie became possessed with a sense of purpose. We quickly got into the zone. Though for me that meant lowering my ambition to not make a fool of myself on film.

Guiding for permit means operating in a time of profound nerves. You have to keep your sport calm in one of the most intense angling equations he'll ever have. Many permit anglers are serious men used to success in their professional lives. When they fall short, as many inevitably do, they don't want to blame themselves so they blame the closest person, the guide. In this particular setting, however, the guide is the unequivocal expert, this is his boardroom, his C-suite office, he's at the top of the masthead. He will not take any shit. He may even secretly enjoy the fact that this man lost his nerve and will return to his Upper East Side townhouse a failure.

Charlie wasn't shy about this fact. His theories were the subject of a privately published book that was helpfully waiting for me in the hotel. During the days we had collectively decided not to fish I had plenty of time to read his thoughts about the shortcomings of his high-profile clients. He was keenly aware of the gap between their self-regard and their lack of angling success. I didn't want to be one of those men. I would not have the consolation of flying back to New York in a private plane to helm a Fortune 500 company.

Far from land our world came into focus. The panga rose and fell in the waves. The curtain was up. The drama had begun. Decisions I had made years, even decades ago, had led to this moment. In this amphitheater was all that mattered. I tried to calm myself. I measured the line and suddenly felt a curious sensation. There was a firm pressure on my lower back. It was Charlie's left hand. He placed it there quite forcefully as if he were ushering me through a revolving door. We stood still and the pressure persisted. This had never happened to me before and has never happened since. I'm not sure if the purpose was to focus my attention or if it was a power play. This laying on of hands was the opposite of calming. I tried not to react. I wasn't sure Charlie knew my name.

Charlie had been clear that I should not strip the crab pattern in—that is, I should not retrieve it in long pulls. *Just tick, tick, tick*, he had said and demonstrated the smallest possible strip, inch by inch, to imitate the movement of a crab which tries to bury itself in the sand. This could be done with only two fingers on the line, he said, which would stop the tendency to grip the line and haul it in in a long pull.

"Now you see that fish," he said, his hand squarely on my back. I did. "Now!" I exhaled and made a bad cast. I quickly gathered myself and cast again right where I aimed. The permit was nearly invisible between the waves. When my fly entered the water the tail disappeared. I was sure I'd spooked the fish and that was that. All this, all the miles, all the dreaming, all the hands on all the backs, everything was over in an instant.

Another wave rose and suddenly we could see the entire body of the permit. It was at our eye level; the silver flank, a wide, brilliant sail. It moved with purpose, diving down toward my fly. This was it. *Holy shit!* My stomach turned.

My rod was straight ahead, as it should be. And I held the loose fly line with my opposite hand. Suddenly I felt a tiny knock in the line. The permit! Then nothing. What? No. Impossible. Had any of that really happened? I was disoriented. Slightly sickened, I tried to collect my thoughts in silence.

This tranquil state did not abide.

"*Motherfucking permit!*" Charlie exploded. He slapped the water with both his hands. "*Damn it. Damn it, permit. Christ!*" Charlie howled. I wasn't sure what emotional trajectory our group was on. "He missed it. He went for the crab." Charlie was apoplectic. "He just missed the crab, that fucker!"

The timbre of these remarks took me by surprise. Charlie had not raised his voice to this point or indicated a passionate hidden nature. On the contrary, he seemed to take pride in his own indifference to any success I might enjoy. His anger had the surprising effect of calming me down. I wanted to reassure him. It wasn't *that* bad. This diatribe had been delivered entirely to the permit. But Charlie turned around. Now he looked at me.

"Did you strip the fly?" he asked calmly. The photographer was watching. The assistant was watching. I was quiet as I prepared my response. "The crab. Did you tick, tick, tick, like I told you?" He paused. "Or did you strip it in? Which I told you no." If this was a cross-examination, I felt like a hostile witness. I looked down at my hands as if they would provide an answer. "No?" I answered, my voice tailing up. "I ticked, ticked. Just like you said." I didn't know if I had, in the excitement of the diving permit, made a fateful strip, trying to set the hook. But I was standing by my story.

That was the only fish we saw. After a choppy ride home, we went to a tarpon spot that was resolutely free of fish. The photographer got some shots of me casting toward nothing. We returned to the dock. "If you want to catch a tarpon then come in April," Charlie said flatly. This was November. Good to know. Thanks, Charlie. Have a good winter.

The fishing on that trip was, it had to be said, disastrous, only two casts to fish. The hotel, the Turtle Inn, conversely, was great, so I arranged a return visit with my family. This would also allow me to fish for a few days and set things right. This was closer to late spring, when the fishing was apparently better, and with a different guide, Elloy, this might be a better angling marriage.

This trip was unusual for me because I would be with my family. I'm close with my parents and sister. But we've also come to an agreement, largely unspoken, that my fishing shall remain distinct from traveling we do together, an angling separation of church and state. This has served all parties well. None of the anxiety that can surge through a fishing trip overlaps into relaxing on the beach. My family is not emotional collateral damage from the lows of an angler who's been in direct sun for eight hours with nothing to show for it. In short, they are happy not to know what a permit is. I wasn't sure how much to tell them.

BELIZE

In Belize we'll celebrate my dad's birthday with a low-key agenda. My sister enjoys papaya and lime for breakfast. My mom destroys detective novels, my sister works the crossword, my dad paints watercolors. I try to crack some *Times* acrostics I've been hoarding. We eat grilled fish and drink white wine with ice cubes

The days are breezy. Quite windy in fact. Sargassum piles up on the beach overnight, where it's raked away by the hotel staff as the sun comes up. I hesitate to note that these are not ideal fishing conditions. When you explain the stakes to a civilian everything sounds foolish. There's no easy way to say: I want to catch a permit which is nearly impossible and yet I'll be disappointed in my performance and depressed with myself afterward. Happy birthday, Dad!

The night before my fishing expedition I feel compelled to explain to my loved ones what a permit is. Photos may have been involved. My sister, Sarah, can't get over the mouth of this fish. I realize I haven't mentioned that yet. I want you to think highly of the permit. I want you to revere the fish the way I do. The permit's mouth makes that more difficult. It looks, with a pink fleshiness, like the lips of a person. It's unsettling.

I'm leaving the easygoing life at the Turtle Inn, where I can sit in the shade, drink an aged rum collins, read Philip Kerr novels, and think pleasing thoughts. Why would I give that up, head over to the marina and enter the gauntlet of fly fishing?

Logic has nothing to do with it.

* * *

I sleep on a large teak bed beneath a ceiling fan, wake up early, and peer through the slatted doors. Outside there's no wind, the water is dark and flat. The day is calm. I smile; the weather has turned in our favor. This feels rare, as anglers, some of the world's great paranoiacs, are convinced they're at the short end of endless meteorological conspiracies.

I eat fried eggs and toast, the sun is already up. I walk with two rods, my waterproof bag, across the road and onto the pier on the lagoon. I meet Elloy. He's a thin man with a short gray beard, like Bill Russell's. But a foot shorter, maybe two, than the legendary Celtic. He has a reluctant but broad white smile, boyish and wise. Elloy maintains a sense of curiosity that many great guides possess. This doesn't feel like a psychologically fraught situation. We'll get to the permit-induced soul searching soon enough.

I know he's assessing me. What type of person am I, have I done this before, will I be good company, all the things that you want to know about somebody you'll be on a boat with for hours. We speak easily but warily. "And what do you want to do today?" he asks. It seems impossibly bad luck to mention a grand slam, much less declare my intentions for a permit.

"Well," I hear myself say, "I'm up for anything. Of course, I'd like a chance at a permit or a tarpon. And I still love bonefish. But I'm in your hands." This seems diplomatic and has the added benefit of being more or less true. I want to be realistic—this is Elloy's territory and he knows what's been fishing well. On the other hand, let's be ambitious! I didn't come to Belize to catch another bonefish.

We head down the channel past docks and people preparing their boats in the morning. Elloy waves to friends and they speak quickly in a strong dialect. We come around the point past the Placencia dock and head east across the bay. By 7 a.m. the sun is hot. We run forty-five minutes to the keys. This is the most relaxing time of the day. The ride is pure pleasure. The intensity comes later.

I revisit my previous permit failures and feel like a minor-league baseball player called up to the majors, who wasn't ready for the show. I couldn't hit the curve. In trout fishing the cast is methodical and repeated. You cast to where trout are rising or in logical places where they hold. There are nervy moments when you have one chance at a fish, but you have developed some sense of rhythm when you make your fateful cast.

Not with permit fishing. You wait and wait, holding your line until after five minutes or three hours, the permit makes a sudden appearance. Often just a cameo. If the fish is swimming, then the boat has to head toward it so you can intersect its path with a cast. But the permit is a great changer of directions. If that happens, the cast has to be picked up and reestablished at a different distance and angle. All quickly, all accurately. Just writing about this makes me nervous.

These are the same principles as casting to bonefish. But there are many bonefish and they're agreeable. There are not many permit and they're particular. There's the rare and wonderful situation when a permit is tailing. It puts its flattened nose in the sand to find a crab, tilts down and its fanlike tail comes out above the water, clearly visible. Then you try not to have a heart attack.

Now you wade or the guide poles the boat and keeps you as far as possible from the permit while you can still make an accurate cast. In these moments you're certain the permit will leave. You may be more certain than about anything in your life. The agonizing urgency is so intense that you want whatever is going to happen to happen. Just blow everything up and go straight to the agony. It's the waiting that kills you.

The angler overestimates his ability and wants to cast too early. The guide tells you to wait. In slow motion you make your approach and uncoil a cast. And that cast fails you. Not close enough. If you're lucky the permit continues blithely unaware of cast number one. But it's hard to make a cast number two because now you're so tense you feel like you're going to explode. Next time you'll put it right on the nose. But no! This cast is too close. The permit flees, and you've never felt so alone.

Let's say you make a good cast. Now you have to gather yourself and, in a wholly different mode and motion, start the tick, tick, tick that Charlie preached, so carefully and so slowly. Some people make a large first strip to get the permit's attention before the small strips. But that can backfire too. The pressure to resolve the situation is unbearable. The permit turns toward the fly, *he's coming for the crab!* And, in a moment of enthusiasm, you strip the crab again, this time fatefully too far and the permit loses interest. You have to start over. From the beginning.

• ❀ •

Elloy and I stop near an island where the water is dark tropical blue. The hole is so deep we can see down where bonefish and, hopefully, permit will be feeding. Elloy asks me to cast toward a cloud of sand and let the line sink. I strip, feel a resistance, reel in, and land a small bonefish. It's like a teenage bonefish, not large enough to make a proper run.

This isn't as fun as catching bonefish in shallow water. This lacks the visual experience which makes the sport great. I cast some more and land a few small ones, but this is missing a certain charge. Catching small bonefish out of deep water is not what I want to do. Sometimes guides want you to catch one fish, any fish, before getting more ambitious. Like card players eager to win their first hand, to *get off the schneid*. Elloy and I come to an understanding. Enough teenage bonefish.

Darker shapes move nearby. "There go the permit," Elloy says. They're right below the boat, but deep down, casually going on about their day as if they aren't one of the most sought after fish in the world. They're living their permit lives, indifferent to the fact that we're dreaming about them. Do they know how much they're coveted? We watch these permit with no fraught desire. They're fish in beautiful water, swimming in pairs. These permit aren't feeding, they won't be caught. But now we know they're here.

The permit stay away so we decide to have lunch. With no wind it's hot in the sun. Elloy lifts the awning over the boat's bench and we sit side by side and gaze out at the water. It's an oddly intimate arrangement. Elloy tells me about his studies with a researcher from Texas A&M who comes to Belize every year. They look for breeding grounds for tarpon and permit. He's easygoing and knowledgeable, and this feels different from our relationship while fishing.

As we head back toward Placencia I feel slightly dejected. We just haven't seen a lot of fish. Our day is almost over but Elloy has a plan. I swear the typical blood oath to keep it to myself. In this secret place are baby tarpon. They come into the shallows as the water cools and the sun starts to set. I cast a Purple Bunny and quicky hook four small tarpon and land a couple over ten pounds. After Cuba I fight a tarpon more comfortably. It's nice to catch a fish, of course, and it's nice to feel like I've learned something. I look forward to the stripe of black along the tarpon's black, like a streak of oil. The day is redeemed with late action, the correct order of things. Long drawn out nothing, then end on a high. Elloy is excited for the next day and so am I.

I return to the hotel. My parents and sister are right where they were, perfectly relaxed. I swim. We have dinner on the beach. Grilled shrimp with lime and a terrific creole stew. There's one more day to fish.

The weather remains calm the next morning. Elloy and I have a sense of what to do. Well he has a sense and I agree immediately. We return to the secret place from the previous afternoon. The tarpon are waiting. One quickly takes my fly. There's always a question about when the tarpon will jump. You reel hard against their strength, the line barely coming, then suddenly there's no pressure and the fish bursts into the air. Thrilling. You have to give back line or the fish will break off your fly when it lands. The easiest way to do this is to lean forward while the fish is in the air — you *bow*, as they say, toward the tarpon, pointing your rod toward the water.

This tarpon doesn't waste any time and immediately jumps. It's five feet in the air and it shakes a long white stomach at us. The lightest part of this fish is right in my face. Elloy howls with laughter and I land a respectable (for me) twelve-pounder. The record-holders would not dream of getting involved with a fish like this. Ten minutes later I've landed tarpon number two. And catching a couple of tarpon by 8 a.m. is already a good day for me. I imagine my family waking up and sitting down to papaya.

Around the bend is the rarest of all sights — a group of permit. We see tails — dark, iridescent, pointing out of the water. They're feeding. I try to keep my nerve. Part of me tries to cast to the permit as if they were bonefish. The angling equivalent of imagining an audience naked in black socks. That doesn't work. The permit retreat and circle back toward the boat. After the requisite bad casts I make a good one.

But a good cast is only part of this journey. The fish has to see the crab. And of course he has to take it, as I remember from my previous permit odyssey. Then, and this is when you feel like you're going to melt with anxiety, you have to set the hook. I try to think about the big picture. But the big picture is too big to comprehend. So: a cast. A permit moves directly and takes the fly. This is happening. I feel a momentary pressure on the line—the permit has taken the fly. It's actually there. I strip and set the hook.

For a brief second there's the weight of the fish. Then the line goes slack. I'm sickened. I strip in line and pick up the fly. There's barely any fly left. The crab is destroyed. What? I look closely. In utter despair I realize the hook broke. Near the eye. No. This is impossible. This is insanity. This is winning the lottery and getting hit by lightning as you cash your ticket. A broken hook is the wrath of a vengeful god. This is a new way to lose a permit.

I am now part of the noble fraternity of depressed anglers who have been separated from permit in a manner previously unimaginable. I envision myself in old age wandering remote islands, long white beard, mumbling to alarmed strangers, "Belize . . . lost permit . . . broken hook." This is the agonizing way the Vikings lose in the playoffs. You text your friends, *I'm done with this team.* Or the classic: *I hate sports.* Right now, in the face of this cruelest of fates, I'm afraid to say, *I hate fishing.* Who would willingly put themselves through this torture? It's emotional mayhem. Complete madness. King Lear on the water.

I try to come to terms with this distinction. I want to laugh, but can't bring myself to appreciate the dark comedy of the moment. Elloy tries to sympathize but we both know there's nothing he can do. Later he says: "Don't strip to set the hook, let the permit set itself."

I tie on another crab pattern and try to escape the cloud of self-pity casting a shadow across my soul. To my surprise a group of permit returns to feed. I make another cast toward a cruising permit. Quickly, perfectly naturally, a fish swims in a direct line and takes the fly. This happens so fast I can't capsize the situation with a premature set. Before anything can go wrong, the fish is on and the permit tears away from the boat.

My reel howls as line pulls out. I briefly feel good. Or at least not dreading what could possibly go wrong. "Raise the rod!" Elloy yells. What? I'm already holding the rod up. But he wants me to hold my arms all the way above my head to keep the line out of the water. "Don't get caught on the coral!" Yes, coral, that would be bad. Do not lose this fish by breaking the leader on coral. Noted. Most bad things that happen fighting a saltwater fish happen right away. Once the fish has gone on its first run and the line is on the reel, you're in a good place. Not this time. Losing this fish would be a full-fledged catastrophe.

I'm fighting a permit in Belize. I don't even know who I am. I'm in an alternate reality, intensely aware of all that can go wrong. Elloy poles after the fish and the permit is beyond the reef and suddenly we're in deep water. This is good, our boat is away from the flats and there's nothing for the line to catch on. I look into blue with no end.

The permit is strong and once it's in depth the fish goes all the way down. And I mean down. My rod bends double and the fish takes out fly line into the backing (reserve line on the reel for these vital moments). You don't see your backing that often—it means you're fighting a serious fish—and you don't want to think too hard about the stability of some knot tied years ago.

Suddenly I notice slight but unmistakable threads fraying in a few places. If the backing disintegrates there will be no way to recover and it will be straight to the hotel bar. Forget that, I'm not sure I'll even return to land. In Thomas McGuane's phrase about losing a permit, I'll be *ready for the rubber room*. But the backing holds. I focus on other issues. Notably that my rod is bent entirely into the water. I imagine it snapping under the pressure and wonder, *They test for these situations, right?*

My mind goes to strange places. I'm possessed with an awareness of what losing this fish would mean. Human error has, for once, been avoided; if there's a mechanical error, I'll have to be institutionalized far from saltwater. Now that we've made it out here, Elloy seems calm. "We're in good shape," he says. I try to internalize this. But I still haven't seen the fish. Now I look down, and the permit's side shines bright silver far underwater. A plane of reflecting light, a brilliant kite, a hundred feet down, set against the deepest blue.

The permit starts to tire, this has been ten minutes, maybe more, maybe less, my grip on reality is not lucid. The area of engagement is close to the boat. Elloy moves off the platform and stands near me. As the permit comes close I lift the rod and lead the fish alongside the panga. Elloy reaches down and in one motion grabs below the tail, makes a fist, and pulls the fish up.

Elloy holds the permit, bright silver, between us. Elloy whoops. I'm too stunned to speak, my mouth is open, but I have no words. Elloy says the fish is twelve pounds (probably ten, nothing to scoff at). I hold the fish upright in the water. The permit is not as narrow as I thought. The dorsal fin is slightly curved and comes to a point, like a scythe. The back is firm and hard, a wonderful, strong fish.

Now Elloy holds the permit by the tail and pulls it back and forth in the water until it revives. Then he lets the tail go and the permit swims straight down into deep water until we can't see it anymore. We don't embrace. But I would happily hug Elloy. Who can understand this who hasn't been through it? My family will be happy for me in the sense that they're happy when I'm happy. I will always have a connection with Elloy. We caught my first permit together. That's worth celebrating. I open a beer. Elloy holds himself more naturally, probably the way he is when he's not working. I imagine I'm different too. Caring about something too much is ridiculous and yet we persist. Under the bright sky, my world is new.

It's 11 a.m. I've never done more before noon in my life. We've caught tarpon and a permit, by far the most difficult parts of the grand slam. We have the rest of the day to catch a bonefish. No problem. But the bonefish are a long run from where we are. Do I really want to go all that way to catch one of those little bonefish? What does that prove? There are still permit feeding back on the reef. What's more important? The grand slam or the chance at another permit? I test out a theory about having caught a bonefish the previous day, so I did catch a grand slam within twenty-four hours. But it doesn't work that way.

Watching the permit swim away is one of the most wonderful things I've seen, the silver fish turning darker as it disappears into the blue. "Whatever you want to do," Elloy says. What could be better than what we're doing? The appeal of a grand slam is real, but there are permit nearby. "Let's stay," I finally say. "The permit are here. Let's keep fishing." Elloy smiles. "Sounds good." We know the odds are against us as we return to the shallows and I get back on the deck.

We didn't catch another permit that day. But neither of us knew that as we looked across the water and I got ready for the next cast.

CHAPTER IV

NORWAY

Dubious Distinction

My desire to catch a salmon is so intense it embarrasses me. It makes me uneasy—wanting something too much leads to bad things. This state of irrationality makes me nervous. But I should admit my salmon devotion and accept the consequences.

Salmon go hand in hand with reverence and, conversely,

heartbreak. They're unlike any other fish—any other animal, really. Maybe that's why I believe, against the evidence, that catching one will change my life. I don't know how, maybe I'll understand the old ways or gain some perspective. Strong emotions can't always be explained with words; like music, they exist outside language.

My salmon debut arrived a few years ago, at a private club in New Brunswick where I had the distinction of catching the smallest recorded fish in their history. The fish in question was a grilse, a young salmon that has yet to head out to the ocean, not the mature fish most anglers seek. The grilse of note was two and three-quarter pounds, if you must know, and the guide, showing a bracing lack of hospitality, made sure I understood that this was no three-pound grilse. In theory, one grilse is better than no grilse. But I've spent the intervening years wondering if the smallest grilse is somehow worse than no grilse.

Despite this undignified introduction, salmon fishing gripped me. I was attracted to the old lodges and the named pools on legendary rivers, the anglers returning the same week, year after year, reconnecting with the flinty guides and using the traditional flies their grandfathers used. All for the chance at a fish they have good odds of *not* catching. The reason is the salmon itself: strong, silver, brilliant, the fish of a thousand casts. In theory all of these elements come together in a remarkable convergence—the ultimate long shot. *I can be patient*, I told myself. *For salmon I can wait.*

To understand salmon is to be in awe. The salmon lives in freshwater and saltwater. A salmon at sea can swim thousands of miles, avoiding sharks and seals, boats and nets, itself a great feat. The salmon lives large, turns bright, grows strong, and is rewarded with an oceanwide banquet—shrimp, krill, herring, and more—sometimes diving three thousand feet to feed. They need all this because when they return to the river on their migratory journey against the current they will not eat.

Then salmon gather at the mouth of the river until there's enough water to start up it. Nobody knows when the salmon will begin their demanding trip. But the salmon know. They come to this place, after their time across the Atlantic called by an innate sense of smell and a relationship to the earth's magnetic fields. This seems cosmically impossible but is incredibly real. They swim many miles upstream to spawn, sometimes to the exact same pool where they were born. The cycle continues.

As I get older, migrations feel more poignant, they make me emotional. Am I getting sentimental in middle age? I'm aware of a wider purpose—salmon have been performing this ancient ritual for millions of years. Their movements are carved into time more deeply than ours. Their runs are staggered, they come up the rivers at different times, to better guarantee the survival of their line. Miraculous. But not so miraculous, unfortunately, that they are indefinite. Salmon runs are decreasing, an indictment of the greed, indifference, and environmental mismanagement that defines our age. Healthy rivers have healthy salmon and those are harder to find. That makes this a bittersweet pursuit. There's no way to fish for salmon without being aware of this increasingly fragile equation.

I hope that as I get older salmon will be part of my fishing life. I want to get on the path and pay my respects. I want to catch and land one salmon, then let it go. And, I realize that these are famous last words: I want one good chance.

My record-setting grilse was caught on a narrow river where I cast the 8wt rod I use for bonefish. The rivers in Norway are larger, some are immense. Anglers use two-handed rods and a casting technique called a Spey cast. They stand right against a raised bank without catching the trees behind them, while casting a great distance in a compact motion. Neat, right?

Not so fast. This sweeping, lovely Spey cast looks easy when pulled off by an expert. Learning to Spey cast, even for a seasoned angler, can be humbling. As I started my Spey casting journey, I made mistakes I thought were behind me. Muscling the rod, moving too quickly, being impatient. I'm no master caster with one hand, but am adequate for most of what I need to do. Spey casting put all that in sharp relief.

My first mistake was calling it a Spey cast. It's really a double-hand cast, one technique of which is called a Spey (there are others). This rod is long, usually between twelve and fifteen feet, hands held on cork grips about a foot apart. This long rod generates power in a slow looping motion that swings the fly line along the water, creating surface tension before it's flicked, across the water fifty feet, eighty feet—for experts, more than a hundred feet. When done correctly this looks majestic and, to be honest, not that hard. Back on earth it's hard as hell.

To cast something a great distance, our first instinct is to propel it with force. Like throwing a ball as far as you can. This instinct causes considerable distress and unhappiness among people learning to cast double-hand rods. It's not strength that's the key, but other factors. You need the right amount of line on the water, which you swing around you at the correct speed, before releasing a surprisingly concise two-handed flick that propels the line across the river. You'll see an old-timer struggle to get into the water, but once he's there his cast keeps going and going, and he looks like a goddamn angling god. A cast to give us all hope.

I first learned to double-hand cast in Paramus, New Jersey, not a famed salmon destination. A man who runs a fly shop in town (really a strip mall on a highway), took me to a wide river with brown water off the Jersey Turnpike. You have to start somewhere. I tried to graduate from amateur to acceptable while rush hour traffic crossed a bridge overhead.

This was a few years ago, while dutifully preparing for a steelhead trip to British Columbia. After my instruction I wasn't bad. Once I arrived in Canada and tried to cast to actual fish, I realized I was closer to bad than good. I cast six feet short of wherever the fish were. One iron law of angling: The fish are always farther away. Trying to compensate, unfortunately, makes things worse. You can't just try harder, it's not a question of effort. Thankfully we ended up on a smaller river and I managed to cast far enough and right in front of a willing steelhead to my amazement and eternal happiness. I sat on the riverbank with my friends and toasted the fish with a can of something called a Caesar, a bloody Mary with Clamato, a Canadian specialty. No dubious drink ever tasted better.

For this trip to Norway, I had to improve. A friend, a ferociously competent salmon angler, offered to help me with my cast. We stood side by side on the Delaware River in the Catskills, and, following his guidance, I started to feel better about things. Between casts, he took the opportunity to divulge certain angling opinions, some unflinching. "Trout fishing, done correctly, requires skills that take years to master," he intoned. I'm susceptible to declarative fishing talk as assurance inspires confidence in a realm full of uncertainty.

"Salmon fishing is different," he continued as I listened closely. "It requires swinging the line, and if you can cast far enough then you can succeed almost by accident." He was warming up. "Even an idiot can catch a salmon." This didn't seem like the time to clarify that I hadn't caught a mature Atlantic salmon. I wondered if, in his formulation, that made me less than an idiot.

Over the following days, I realized I didn't care exactly how I landed this hypothetical salmon. I didn't need a perfect cast, I didn't need the salmon to take a dry fly and theatrically jump, while I fought it beautifully. The process didn't have to be picturesque. I could catch any salmon even if chance played its part. No, I declared to myself, *I don't care if I'm lucky. I don't care if I'm unworthy. All that matters is that I catch a salmon and land it.*

I will go to Norway. I want to be that idiot.

NORWAY

• • •

The Alta is the most famous river in Norway and the greatest salmon river in the world. A week's fishing on the Alta costs as much as a small car. Beyond the cost, you have to know somebody who can get you on. Like playing a round at Augusta National, you need money, but you really need an in. Heading to Norway for the first time I am most definitely *not* fishing the Alta. So let's get rid of that notion right away.

My casting friend gave me the name of a Swedish expert who might advance my salmon education. Every summer this man, a well-known designer of rods and salmon tackle, crosses the border into Norway to teach anglers from around the world how to fish for salmon. He's a legendary caster and has a special method. His name is Johan.

I email Johan and enroll in his salmon academy. This school is based in an old wooden house Johan rents on the Sanddøla River, a large tributary of the even larger, more famous Namsen. There are a few hours of instruction each day, the rest of the time I can fish on the beats Johan reserves for students. Lodging is provided, everybody prepares their own meals.

Organized activities with strangers can be deadly. Like any sane person, I avoid situations requiring nametags. But this school will make me a better caster in an incredible setting where I can fish. That Johan, I gather from my friend, is a mercurial personality does not deter me. If anything, I flatter myself that I can handle a tough love approach.

Johan maintains his mystique through an elusive

approach to correspondence. Replies to my emails come after five minutes or five weeks. If Johan is trying to build intrigue, he doesn't have to bother. I'm completely in the bag. I'm ready to go to Norway. I will learn from a master and I will catch my salmon.

What could possibly go wrong?

This, I declare to myself, will be one of the last great quests I make as an angler. I'm given to this type of proclamation every few years. As a teenager I thought my life would be complete when I passed my driver's license test (life continued roughly as before, just slightly farther from home). My friends used to want to get into sold-out concerts—now they swear all they want is their kid to get into the right preschool. These things evolve, but just like insisting all you want is to cast to a permit, it's never enough. Never believe anybody who says this is the only thing they want.

Except this time. Because this is it. I don't want to say I'm running out of fish, but salmon is the big one. Catching a fish won't teach you how to live, but you might have a moment of clarity when you accomplish what matters to you. It's clear to me what I will do: I will catch a salmon in Norway and be granted eternal wisdom and never ask for anything again. All right, I still want my Minnesota Vikings to win the Super Bowl. But if the Vikings win the Super Bowl then I'll know we're living in a simulation. No, the Vikings winning is too much to ask. The salmon will have to do.

* * *

I prepare for this quest, naturally, by properly outfitting myself. Over the years, I've amassed a deep collection of trout and saltwater equipment. What I bring on the water is drawn from a considerable archive strategically located in various closets, car trunks, club lockers, and duffel bags across the East Coast and moving west to our cabin in Wisconsin. This is all carefully tracked and marshaled by me according to the seasons, with the precision of classified documents.

Salmon tackle is a new world. Starting with a Spey rod and reel with a specific line that floats, one that sinks slowly, and another that sinks less. I'll be forced, *forced*, to purchase an arsenal of flies. Many salmon flies have high wings, so I need new, taller fly boxes to keep them from getting crushed. I text Ruaridh in Havana for guidance. Not only is he a salmon expert, but as a Scotsman his advice is fiscally prudent.

Salmon flies have no relationship to trout flies. Their names are different, so are their sizes and silhouettes. They sink, they skitter, they float. Remember, salmon aren't feeding when they're migrating up the river. They react— out of annoyance or instinct—and take your Black Ghost, your Ally's Shrimp, your Green Bomber. Though most likely they don't take anything of yours. So depending on your point of view the fly choice is of utmost importance or totally random.

On eBay I find a handsome old Wheatley box full of tube flies that belonged to an Englishman, who may or may not have slipped this mortal coil. I order flies from Doak & Sons, located, naturally enough, in Doaktown, where I stopped en route to my grilse adventure in New Brunswick. I buy single flies from experts and boxes at discount. I'm bringing in the best minds here. I buy a handsome Swedish reel that's too expensive, but I know that if I use it to land my first salmon then I will love it even more.

In 1971, my parents drove for days up to the Norwegian fjords when they lived in Europe after college. They were planning to camp but it rained and they ended up staying in charming hotels in old wooden houses. They still talk about that trip warmly. My mom describes immense maps, each representing a band of the country, which they bought at gas stations every hundred miles as they drove north off the map they were using. She navigated as my dad drove their brown MG, a car I can't believe they owned.

Things are easier these days. The good people at Volvo loaned me a handsome XC90, a more modern version of my fishing mobile, which is parked back home and still has a CD player in the dash. Into this modern car, I load my duffel bag, which weighs an extraordinary forty pounds (the weight of a good salmon on the Alta). I feel like I should drop off Scandinavian children at soccer practice. Its digital navigation is discreetly projected onto the windshield, intuitive and helpful. There's something strange about the power digital maps have over my life. I'm a captive of convenience and don't appreciate the lay of the land as I would if I used a physical map. At least I don't get lost.

My trip begins in Sweden, a country so orderly that it makes me feel orderly. Looking out of my hotel window in Stockholm I see rows of people dutifully bicycling to work, women, men, old, young. I visit Östermalm, the covered food market, with stalls full of vegetables, stolid butchers with their steaks, and of course, fishmongers, with salmon, so silver, laid out on ice. Everything feels elegant and correct, like I'm going to dinner at the grandmother's house in *Fanny and Alexander*. I head to Lisa Elmqvist, a restaurant that began eighty years ago when young Lisa sold fish from a stall. I sit at the civilized bar and order a lake pike with some fall mushrooms.

I drive west and north. All border rivalries are broadly the same, but the specifics differ. There's friendly friction between Sweden and Norway. Sweden was traditionally more prosperous—they had industry and Norway had farms. Then Norway discovered natural gas and everybody made money. Prices are so high that Norwegians do their shopping in Sweden. There are accusations of snobbishness and superiority. I do remember, years ago, an article that said the Swedes were not offended by the Swedish Chef on *The Muppet Show*. Why would they be? they asked. It was quite clear he sounded Norwegian.

In case there's any doubt you've entered Norway, there's a thirty-foot troll looming at the border. I drive north past Lillehammer and see signs from the old Olympics. I always root for the Norwegian cross-country ski team, which sends people over just to wax the skis. You're born on skis,

they say in Norway, and these people love to be outside—
nearly every car has a roof rack for skis or bicycles.

Directed by my digital map—I would do whatever this
map tells me short of driving into the river—I leave the
highway and head up a dirt road past some healthy pale
brown cows. Everything seems healthy in Norway, everybody looks like they hiked hours in the sunshine to meet
you. I arrive at the Budsjord, a farm from the 1700s, a series
of handsome dark wood buildings around a green yard.
Summer farms were built to take the animals up in warm
months where they could eat grass and the owners could
enjoy the cool air. When the weather got cold, they went
back down to their homes in the fields along the river.

I'm greeted by Elspeth, who radiates good health and the
general virtue of the area. She shows me around the property, one incredible wooden building after another, perfectly restored and maintained by an architect from Oslo.
My cabin has wooden furniture, as expected, well done, a
stone fireplace, a few old photos of a handsome unsmiling
couple, and windows with views across the valley. The beds
are made beautifully, with the rolled eiderdowns, as they
often are in Scandinavia.

"Do you eat venison?" Elspeth asks. I'll eat whatever
they serve in this special place. "Dinner is at 6 p.m. I start
the fire at 5 p.m." There's an incredible stone fireplace—
really the corner of the dining room. They are serious about
fires and firewood here. On the drive I passed artful stacks
of wood outside farmhouses. The wood is cut specifically
and stored carefully and there are theories, opinions, and
strong disagreements, about every aspect of the process.

There was a TV show that just showed a fire being maintained that caused outrage among viewers convinced they were doing it wrong.

We are on the pilgrim's trail, where people take strenuous hikes and stay, usually with their own sleeping bags, in outbuildings at hotels spread throughout the mountains. Some hike all the way from Trondheim, over two hundred kilometers. People on this pilgrimage leave each morning for the next leg of their trip, regardless of the weather, aching muscles, or other attachments. I see a young woman wrapping her foot. "My boots fell apart," she says. "I have to wear new ones that aren't broken in yet." She has twelve kilometers uphill the next day.

At dinner I meet a few pilgrims and feel sympathy with them. Everybody is active in Norway. "Summer is so short here we can't waste time," one says. Soon the days get dark. "I start to get sad in November," she confesses. I wonder if they're looking for the same things I want. Solitude? An improbable achievement? Or something different?

It's hard to leave Budsjord the next morning. What a perfect place to read and write and eat by the fire. I discover that hotels in Norway, however small, make their own jam and usually their own bread. Good yogurt, mild cheese from the brown cows. Sometimes herring if you're ready for that first thing. There's a tradition of bringing food with you for your day hiking or driving. Pocket food they call it, and there's even paper to wrap it. You pull off the highway to one of the many picnic tables with benches and views into the country and enjoy your smoked salmon and brown bread.

It's late August, after the summer holiday. There are fewer campers on the road than usual, I'm told, though there seem like many to me. The gas stations sell bratwurst and kielbasa. People have no problem eating them bright and early, which strikes me as aggressive. My feeling is that gas stations and meat don't play well together, especially before noon. But people say the best fried chicken in America is from gas stations down South, so who knows? I'm willing to remain in the dark.

Driving north past Trondheim the roads get less crowded. The river grows wider. I'm getting closer.

I pull up to Johan's house outside the town of Grong, late in the afternoon. He lumbers outside and we shake hands. His eyes are a gentle blue, that I suspect is misleading. He's eighty-something years old, walks with a limp, and doesn't wade much anymore. Yet he must have been formidable in his younger days. He speaks in such a rounded Swedish accent in unhurried English that it takes time to realize his sharp opinions are often at my expense. He's happy to laugh, usually at his own remarks. "My neighbor's shithouse is older than your country," he howls.

You don't know what your expectations are until you arrive at a destination, when romance comes into contact with life's mundane realities. Johan's rented house, where I'm staying for the week, is jangly and charming, though it gets less charming the farther I go into it. My room—the only carpeted room in the house—recalls a 1970s dormitory. A rather suggestive Gustav Klimt poster hangs over the bed. I expected the requisite print of the angler in a landscape and the feeling of an old, neglected inn. There's a black leather chair, leatherette in fact, that must have made its debut a few decades ago in an Oslo bachelor apartment. I wasn't counting on the artfully preserved Budsjord. But this is more incongruous than I imagined.

Apparently I will be the academy's lone student, the others have canceled or rescheduled. We're still recovering from a pandemic, after all, and travel plans change. This strikes me as a good thing. Wisdom will be handed down in a straight line, undiluted, from Johan to me.

At our first session, Johan asks me to set up my rod. We're on the porch that runs the length of the house. I fit the sections together and hand him the rod. "Hold the tip," he instructs. I do as he says. He points the rod handle at an angle and it bows deeply. He looks intently up and down the rod and turns the handle the other direction with more pressure.

He arrives at a verdict. "No." He sets the rod on the table rather harshly. "Who made this rod?" I tell him. Johan shakes his head as if the name has unpleasant connotations. "Who told you to buy this?" I pause, I have nobody to blame. "This rod is too fast," he declares. A rod with fast action has more movement at the tip. A slower rod is stiffer and has a stronger, lower section. "This rod is too fast for my technique." He pushes the rod away from him on the table, as if it might infect any other perfectly good rods nearby.

We have six days left together. "What should we do?" I ask. Subpar equipment seems like a manageable part of this equation. I'm more worried about the human element. "I'm happy to borrow a rod, if you have one," I say brightly, knowing he has many rods. There's another pause. "You can use your rod," Johan says flatly. He keeps pushing the rod away, unable to allow it near him. "But to make this rod work your casting has to be perfect."

While I let this sink in, Johan moves on. "May I see your reels." I show him one, made from a company where I believe he used to work. "No," he says. "What is this line?" I explain. "Who told you to get this line?" This was a standard Scandi line. This was starting to feel like a full body exam. "American companies do not understand salmon fishing," he says. I didn't want to get into an international incident. I show him my other reel. "This line is all right. Not perfect, but it will work."

I try to change the topic and say I'm excited to learn to Spey cast. Another wrong move. I should have said that I wanted to learn to double-hand cast. "If you make that mistake in town some of the anglers might lose respect for you." The process of losing respect seemed well underway.

Things settle down and we drive to different beats on the Sanddøla. Johan shows me where I'll be fishing and this is promising. There are gentle riffles, deep pools, and clearings where anglers have stood and caught salmon before. I imagine my first salmon coming from this water. I drop

Johan at the house and head into Grong. I get food and beer in the market and head back to the dorm room, settle in and go to sleep.

I meet Johan every morning at 10 a.m. We sit in the kitchen at a large table and I drink Earl Grey tea (one of the great things named after a person, along with the Clouser Minnow and the Negroni). Johan explains his casting technique with the aid of a small whiteboard. He's an enthusiastic draftsman, and his illustrations with arrows and circles describe the loop that's the basis of Johan's technique. "Master this motion," he says, "and you'll be able to cast any distance."

The clarity of this idea is appealing, like the unifying theory of a cult. Then he sets down his pen and says, ominously, "But you have to understand it." He sounds pensive. "Many people come and learn and they're all right, they're even good." He points to his drawing, which, beneath the arrows, is nearly inscrutable. "But they don't understand it."

He asks a few more questions about force and propulsion and energy. I nod so eagerly that it's clear I don't grasp the principles at stake. This bluff is ill-advised. Then he poses a simple, unexpected question: "Do you understand physics?" I take a moment. If you're asked whether you understand physics then something has gone wrong.

You're asking if I understand physics? That's downright offensive. Do I, a writer, who carefully avoided exposure to the hard sciences in college, understand physics? Outrageous. Of course I understand physics! The gravity apple. Why you can bounce a ball on a moving train. I understand physics, buddy. I understand physics backward and forward. I just don't want to explain theoretical questions about physics to an industrial engineer. I start to worry that this salmon academy might have grades.

Johan wants me to comprehend the motion, not just imitate it. Then it can be adjusted in any situation. Johan's cast is a universal language, master it and become a fluent angler. Johan puts it bluntly. "If you open a book with Greek letters in it, you don't understand shit." This is true. And so far double-hand casting feels like reading Greek.

Our theoretical discussions are over and we head out to the lawn. I cast while Johan watches from a folding chair. "You're pushing," he says, disappointment entering his voice. "You will never cast well if you push with your upper hand." Like many trout anglers I use my dominant hand making the forward push. In Johan's technique the emphasis is on pulling the rod toward you with the bottom hand. Imagine holding a lacrosse stick, which I will also imagine, since I've never held one; the power comes from pulling the lower hand. It doesn't take much effort to create the force that will shoot the line and take your fly to a salmon on the far shore. Though it will take another few hundred more casts to catch a fish.

Johan seems aware of his effect and sugarcoats nothing. In fact he seems to enjoy withholding any sweetener. "For trout fishermen the cast is hard." This makes me feel better; I'm not alone in my struggles. "Some of them never master it. Ever." The good feeling quickly wears off.

• • •

Each afternoon, after class, I go to the Sanddøla. The river is wide and even. Salmon rivers calm me, the signs of drama hidden. Farther down, the river narrows and two channels run between immense rocks. Every salmon in this river must come up those channels. Johan and I see few salmon jump, a large shape bent into a U that floats momentarily above the water. Then it disappears. There's no sound. It's too far away. If you didn't know they were salmon it would feel like your imagination.

A salmon that jumps in fast water will probably keep swimming upstream. That makes it hard to catch. "If it's moving then it just comes down to luck. You don't want to be lucky." I nod. Though who doesn't want to be lucky? When salmon stop, they hold outside the current and rest. Target the salmon where they lie. "You don't want to swing across the entire river," Johan counsels. Focus on fewer, more calculated casts.

Standing alone on the bank of the river, this feels over-whelming. Where do I start? There are some clear targets—large rocks, and a few short runs of softer water near the bank. But the river is huge. I have hours. I tie on a silver-and-blue tube fly that Johan approved. I try not to think about the other hundreds of flies I optimistically acquired that are resting comfortably in boxes with no threat of use. I start with close targets before taking a broader approach. I make some satisfying long casts. I muff some. The wind picks up and I really muff some. I see no more fish. I catch nothing.

I have dinner at the hotel in town. The other option is the gas station, which has a devoted fan base. It's still light after dinner as I head back to the river. This would be easier with a guide or an experienced angler. That's not in the cards. "You should find the fish and catch one yourself," Johan told me earlier. "I don't want to take that experience from you." If I'm honest I don't really care if I take a shortcut. I'll earn this fish through my desire. That, as Johan has drilled into me, is not how things work.

At the liquor store I buy some summer aquavit. It was suggested by the clerk, a sweet older woman who has the air of a librarian. The drink has a faint golden hue and is seasonal and possibly healthful. Back home I head upstairs and open the bottle. Stronger than I was expecting. Some of these farmers just drink all winter, Johan said. They're used to this.

I look around my dorm room. I believe we respond to our surroundings and conduct ourselves accordingly. In the pristine alpine interiors of Budsjord I kept the room clean and immaculate. Here, after a few days, inertia sets in and I've reverted to a more collegiate state. Clothes hang on hooks and doorknobs. Open fly boxes are spread out. There are notebooks, newspapers, and a bag of pretzels. This arrangement will not appear in an interior design magazine.

By the second glass I'm coming around to the aquavit. Pretty good really. I listen to some old Depeche Mode songs and enjoy myself. Drinking in a messy room is teenage behavior. I look in the mirror. My beard is gray, I wear a cardigan more commonly seen on a grandfather. This isn't youthful. This is old. There are wrinkles at the edge of my eyes that are still there when I stop smiling. I'll be sore when I wake up. This is far from the noble pursuit of a salmon. This trip is not translating. I could have driven around Norway with my better half. She would have loved it. What am I doing here?

I'm not expecting to master the cast after a few days. That's not threatening to happen. Sometimes my casting gets better then quickly gets worse. I cast well on the lawn, then go out to the water and watch in horror as a pathetic tangle of lifeless line falls weakly before me. Johan tries to reassure me in his own way. "Don't worry," he says, a rare note of positivity entering his voice. "I should tell you that you're normal." I'm not alone in my struggles. "Only two people learned right away," he says. "A boy, eleven years old, and a woman from Japan."

Johan has been invited to fish all over the world, as a guest and an instructor. He knows exactly how many salmon he's caught and how many weighed more than twenty kilograms. He's met wealthy men and learned from his travels. "It's good to have money," he said one afternoon. "But not too much." After a few days of slow improvement my cast has regressed. Johan asks what day it is. "Wednesday," I tell him. "Wednesday is the day people start to break down," he giggles slightly, as if my mental collapse is amusing to witness. I'm caught between a resentment of Johan's indifference and a perverse desire to please him. When I make a decent cast I turn to him for approval. "Better," he says. "But still not good."

While I cast, Johan talks. "I like honest people. Not all people like somebody who says what they think." Then he expounds upon other theories, some strongly held. "These guides put you on their boat and tell you where to cast." He's getting worked up. I admit to myself that I wouldn't mind being told where to cast. "I have no interest in that. That's barely fishing." This happens, he explains, in famous pools where fish gather before swimming upstream. "You stand there and catch something in narrow water. Who wants this?" I try not to answer.

Learning to fish, at any age, is a balance between technique, principles, and, crucially, results. Johan believes in mastering technique, adhering to principles, and letting the results follow. So far the results are far behind. In the meantime, Johan becomes overwhelmed with emotion. "This is not a lottery!" he explodes. He feels diminished by the prospect of catching a salmon by accident. To that end Johan gives me specific advice for the Sanddøla. Every day he tells me about how to fish the river. Does he secretly want me to succeed?

It's important to plan for success, however remote. We discuss what to do should I catch a salmon on my own. "It's not hard," he says with the sense of calm that comes with having caught over one thousand salmon. "When the fish is tired, just back up onto the bank and beach it." This concerns me. I would have to lay down the rod, walk up to the fish, with no pressure on the line, and grab it below the tail. I tell Johan this seems like a potential disaster. "Once it's on the shore it will stay there. Then," he says clearly, "you have thirty seconds."

The harsh but lovable teacher is such a familiar figure that I'm hesitant to fall for it. In the film version I would get furious with Johan but learn valuable lessons, and his approach would be vindicated when I land a salmon as the sun sets on my last evening. We'd have a farewell handshake and I would invoke his name for the rest of my days. The key to all of this is catching a salmon. At the moment, that's not happening. Johan still takes my questions seriously. He likes discussing how to recognize good lies, how to choose flies, what's the right angle and speed for drifts. He passes a fly over a salmon three times then moves on. "Give the fly movement," he instructs. "Movement is life."

But Johan returns to sharp-edged views. His wrath is directed at shortcuts and the easy way. "You can't buy skill," he says. "You can't guarantee shit." When he senses I'm too focused on results he gets revved up. "You have to trust this process. I'm not a priest," his voice rises. "Do you believe?" he asks. I want to believe, I really do.

Each evening I park at small hut with green plants growing on the roof, in the Norwegian style. There's a rustic, open air gazebo on a low bluff with views down to the river. A freight train passes far up the slope twice each day. I'm getting more familiar with the area. There's a path up and down the river, and now I know how to find the gaps in the bushes where I should cross over.

When I arrive on the bank I feel that this might be the

time. Sometimes I cast from the shallow bank into the widest part of the river. Then I move down and wade into deep water where the current flows by immense rocks. I focus on areas where Johan said salmon might hold. "You need to have a map of the river in your head." I'm getting closer. At night, when it finally gets dark, I go home without success but feel no bitterness.

On the last day, we accept the fact that my casting won't improve. So Johan and I take a leisurely drive around the area. We get in the Volvo, and Johan runs his eyes around the interior. Johan and his wife have been staying in an old camper outside the house, though there's a free bedroom inside. "The bed in the van is fine," he says.

I wonder about Johan and his wife. Fishing is the center of their world. They operate like a political couple whose lives revolve around campaigns. They settled into this pattern long ago when they drove around the countryside all summer and lived in their cabin in the winter. They didn't need more than that. They still don't. I try to imagine driving around Norway with my loved one while I fish for salmon and abandon that idea.

We pass prosperous farms on the quiet side of the river away from the highway. They have paths down to the banks next to wooden signs saying FISHING or just a simple painting of a fish. Salmon fishing is a universal language here. The landowners lease access to anglers, who return year after year. English sportsmen came to Norway in the nineteenth century. They realized this situation was even better than Scotland. They leased the best water, sometimes for decades, and paid the farmers well. They built wooden houses that they painted white where they could stay with their families while fishing for weeks or months at a time. Some are still there, understated, and lovely, known in the area simply as English houses.

Away from instruction, Johan is relaxed. He's come to this valley for more than forty years and points out landmarks and fishing lodges he likes and those run by people he doesn't. Through a clearing we see the river and anglers on boats, some with motors, trolling with spinning rods. Heresy. We cross a bridge and drive over to the Namsen, a vast river, calmly flowing between steep green hills. The water is opaque. No clarity, not what you want. "I've never seen it like this," Johan says somberly. This river flows into the Sanddøla. "I wonder if the fish are waiting for it to clear up."

If that's the case, then there are few salmon running up the Sanddøla. Is this a reprieve? Am I less star-crossed? Is Johan giving me an excuse why I've gone fishless? This is uncharacteristic of the man. Yet there's something odd about the tepid water. I'll never know. Anyway, I'm beyond excuses. The river doesn't feel full of life, but we have seen a few salmon jump.

Fish enough and you'll suffer days injected with hopelessness. This is not that. I'm ready for a burst of action. I know that ten minutes of fighting a fish will put all the previous hours into relief.

Why put myself through this? I could be driving around Norway staying in old farms, eating lingonberries, and living the dream. How do I explain this fiasco to loved ones? Did I expect to come out of this spiritual exercise unscathed? Well, I was scathed. I wanted to be outside the angling equation, more enlightened, beyond the transactional nature of the sport. This trip made a lie of that premise. I fear I need to catch a salmon for my own self-regard. I write Ruaridh to salvage some comedy from the situation. What's the longest he's fished without catching anything? He writes back at once. "I went thirteen days without touching a salmon." I like the phrase "touching a salmon" but don't want to match his record.

I drop Johan at the house. His last words of advice are "Stop pushing so hard." He's referring to my casting motion, though I also interpret that as stop pushing so hard to catch a fish. Desire clouds the situation and you can't see clearly. So much pivots on one fish. One salmon justifies the journey and explains the mysteries behind the motivations. With no salmon I'm not sure what's left.

Angling tragedies I've suffered in the past were dramatic and sharp, like a lightning strike. A fish is on, suddenly, miraculously, and then just as suddenly, the fish is gone. Those were technical disasters; this is thematic. My whole premise is suffering. This salmon situation is laid out unrelentingly and I have hours to reflect on what it means. I want wisdom. Nothing comes.

It's my last night. For the first time I feel real urgency. Everything is still possible, I really do believe. I park the car and prepare as I've done every day. Pull on my waders and my boots, put on my rain jacket to deal with mist that might turn to rain. Assemble my rod, check my knots. If I catch a fish, *my* fish, it will all make sense.

I try to bring to bear what I've learned. Still, the weight of failure will not leave my head. A trip with no salmon becomes folly. When does logic overcome our emotions? That's why they're emotions, our rational side can't control them. The arc of this story is heading down, but I'm not done yet.

Fishing alone you're outside of time. You decide when you're finished. All that matters is how much you care about sleep. But what if, just what if, you catch a salmon after the sun goes down? What a story! This image makes you a prisoner of your own romanticism, of what you know is not just improbable but secretly suspect is impossible. Do you bend to that? Do you give in?

The sky is low and gray. Not a gentle summer evening in northern Europe where the sun lingers at the horizon. Beneath the bank of clouds, a sliver of blue holds out, the thin line of possibility. I still want to rescue the situation. After a few hours of casting rain starts to fall and I climb onto an immense rock, ancient, larger than my living room. I look down along the river around the bend and the water is black.

When you reel in for the last time, you exit the equation. There's no fanciful narrative. It's over. Was it a failure of imagination? Or just a failure? "The art of losing isn't hard to master," Elizabeth Bishop wrote. In losing I keep looking for a secret meaning I can't find. I get to my feet. I head back to the car before it's too dark to see. The rain is supposed to fall through the night. Tomorrow, the salmon will be swimming up the river.

CHAPTER V

SPAIN

Across the Mountain Stream

Angling theory, like religious doctrine, consists of deeply held beliefs, largely unverifiable, that can lead to passionate arguments and strained friendships. Righteousness is rarely attractive, and we don't know how righteous we can be until, our voice rising in strident tones, we defend the dry fly against all that is evil in the world. This is a question of principle and it's important to stand up for what you know is just. Fun, right?

Some of us are forced to confront less historically minded, less patient anglers who resort to Woolly Buggers. These people are *results-based*, that dangerous modern phenomenon. Prioritizing results in fly fishing is often uncomfortable and sometimes impossible—they're not natural bedfellows. Our sport, by design, is not streamlined for success. Fly fishing is like writing longhand rather than typing—it's personal and takes longer. That's why it's nicer to receive a letter than an email, and nicer to catch a fish on a fly than any other way.

The efficiency gurus do not appreciate this sporting balance. Fly fishing isn't supposed to be easy, it's supposed to be hard. Or at least hard enough. And that specific difficulty is how we, in our small way, aim for some higher, if not achievement, at least a higher ideal. This is contrary to the heathenistic impulses of people who can't tell their algorithm from their— wait, I feel a bout of righteousness coming on!

Among fly anglers the most fervently held views concern the dry fly. The dry fly lands on the water and floats. When a trout rises to take it in clear view of the angler, this is the dream. Encouraging a feeding trout to rise to a dry fly during a hatch, when many insects are on the water, is great. To entice a trout to take a dry fly when there are *no* flies around is even greater. So satisfying, in fact, that true believers refuse to resort to a nymph (which drifts underwater) or, heaven forbid, a streamer, which you strip in, even if that's what the trout would be most interested in. The purists make it hard on themselves, because that challenge, and the waiting, justifies the payoff. They prefer one trout on a dry fly to a handful of fish caught any other way. This is serious business.

I thought I knew about dry fly purism. I've fished the chalk streams in England where these rules were invented. There's a clarity that comes with the dry fly ethic, like a dress code. You can't use a nymph on the River Test and you can't wear jeans in the Reform Club. You can get mad or you can accept it. At least you know what's expected of you, which focuses your options. I've been possessed by the dry fly fervor myself—these things come and go. But you don't really know where you fall on a spectrum until you meet people who are so much further out that they need a new spectrum.

Before I went fishing in Spain I associated dry fly fanaticism with ruddy Englishmen with hyphenated last names, not easygoing Latin men who eat dinner at midnight. The anglers I met in Spain, so skilled and stylish, were unlike any I've encountered. It's now clear that I didn't know what purism meant.

This wasn't the obvious way. I was supposed to fish in Sapporo, the northernmost island of Japan, with my friend Taka. Taka is from Tokyo but lives in Florence, where he works for a famous tailor. He's a deadly serious dry fly angler, a true believer. When I tell Taka a fishing story he wants to know if I used a dry fly, and slightly winces if he discovers I caught a fish on a nymph. For Taka it's dry fly or nothing—a policy I admire, if don't practice. You can't argue with these people. They're like vegans.

Our Japan trip was booked, we'd hired a guide, I was really looking forward to the food, honestly, and the fishing was incidental (though we know the fishing is never incidental). The pandemic had other ideas. Travel to Japan was limited and I couldn't get a visa. Apparently trout fishing wasn't considered an emergency activity. Taka and I had some difficult conversations—neither of us wanted to be the first to suggest we cancel. Finally, we faced reality and cashed out. We would live to fish Sapporo another day. Though that day feels very far away.

In the wake of the disappointment, Taka suggested I call his friend Norman. I had met Norman at a party once, but we'd never had dinner together, which I consider the basis of knowing somebody. Not even coffee, the basis for *kind of* knowing somebody. We would soon be on a weeklong fishing trip, which is how you *really* know somebody. Norman was a lawyer who became a shoemaker (a story as old as time), who lived in Barcelona. We arranged to talk.

The fact that we were relative strangers was dawning on me when my phone rang in the Catskills. I answered and the first thing Norman said was: "Did I catch you with your waders on?" As a matter of fact, he had, I was just about to fish. I laughed and knew we'd get along. Then we got down to it. I told him I'd always wanted to fish the mountain streams in the Spanish Pyrenees. This was perfect since Norman knew some of that water and wanted to know more. Within a few minutes we quickly agreed that we'd fish for a week. It all seemed natural.

This might be shocking to somebody who doesn't fish,

and it's somewhat shocking to me. I don't even travel with people I know well. But fishing is different. People who travel to fish already have a lot in common, they are obsessive in a way that I like. Norman and I also saw eye to eye on food and lodging—traditional bars and inns. (I should say his name is pronounced *Nōr-mon*, more dramatic than our English version.)

Norman kindly made the arrangements. All I had to do was show up, which felt luxurious. I would arrive in Barcelona via Madrid, then we'd drive west across the Pyrenees, fishing as we went. Finally, we would descend from the mountains and try our luck on the Irati River. This wasn't a trip to catch a particular fish. Rather, I wanted a larger feeling and Norman agreed. I'd seen photos from Spain of anglers wading in blue streams beneath ancient stone bridges. The idea of leaving the water to have lunch in a medieval tavern—what's not to like? Driving across the Pyrenees felt exciting and rare. Who knew if I'd ever have a chance to fish in Spain again?

Now you might ask, Are there trout in Spain? There are. In *The Sun Also Rises* Jake and Bill go to the Irati for *trout-fishing*, as it's hyphenated in the book. Bill's rods haven't arrived from Scotland so they buy one in a dry goods store in Burguete. That Bill had his rods sent from Scotland to Spain is exciting to me. I would love to casually mention that I'm waiting for my rods to arrive from Scotland. If they don't show up, then I'll just buy a new rod. I'll have no choice. My rods didn't arrive from Scotland.

When Jake first sees the river, he says the water is clear but doesn't look *trouty*. Bill is also skeptical. This is my first encounter with the word "trouty," but I definitely know the feeling of beholding non-trouty water. These are familiar emotions to any angler arriving somewhere new. You read that a river is good, but won't believe it until you catch the first fish.

The two men take different approaches. Bill, who's more patrician, asks skeptically if Jake is *going to fish bait?* Jake indeed plans to fish worms; Bill prefers a McGinty fly. *If they won't take a fly I'll just flick it around.* He'd rather cast a fly than catch a trout on bait. There were tactical disagreements with moral undertones even then. How reassuring.

After fishing they meet in the afternoon and drink wine. Jake has caught half a dozen. *Got them all on worms? You lazy bum.* Bill himself caught three but they were larger, which I suppose gives him the last word. As a boy, I loved this part of the book. That fishing could appear in a novel, almost as if it were smuggled in, excited me. Fishing felt ennobled, part of a better life, like living with a great painting. And the idea of heading off to catch trout in an old country felt thrilling, even illicit.

The Irati, which almost didn't seem real, would be our final stop. First we would fish in the mountains for Mediterranean trout. Norman told me about these small, lovely fish. They resemble brown trout, with dark spots along their sides. I wasn't worried. Just put me below an arched bridge. The fishing, I figured, would take care of itself.

It's morning when I arrive in Madrid. The city is full of storekeepers opening, elegant ladies walking petite dogs, people in cafés lighting their first cigarettes of the day. I cross the Casa de Campo, have a coffee, and shake off jet lag. I head to the Prado, where I haven't been in twenty years. I've always loved Goya and look forward to seeing his paintings.

The Prado is large and stately. It's wonderful returning to a museum after a long time away. This morning everything feels unhurried. I've left the day free and I take my time. Finally, I arrive in a gallery with the black paintings Goya made at the end of his life. I feel their weight and the artist's vulnerability. They're more urgent than I remember. They look menacing, full of a sense of mortality. I leave the galleries unsettled. I feel my age.

On the train to Barcelona the fields turn from gold to green as we get closer to the ocean. There's a book festival throughout the city. The Paseo de Gràcia is lined with stalls and eccentric dealers. Outside bland luxury stores are stacks of novels, art catalogs, dictionaries, manuscripts, prints, paperbacks, maps. The contrast is striking. People browse curiously and there's a cheerful feeling. The printed word strikes back.

Norman's atelier is in an attractive old building on a small square. There are beautiful shoes on display in front and a work area in back, with the distinct short benches, that look like they're from a schoolhouse, where shoemakers sit and shape wooden lasts and build shoes. They make everything from riding boots to loafers, in lovely colors you rarely see—gorgeous green and even purple. These are exquisitely theatrical, not a discreet pair of oxfords.

We have dinner at Bar Cugat, with rounded art nouveau windows, high ceilings, and an easygoing atmosphere. Certain rooms feel better when they're old. Dinner is late here, we sit outside under large oak trees, eat jamón and tortillas and drink wine. Norman's girlfriend is bemused by our fishing trip. It's clear some craziness underlies our endeavor. To her, these fishing trips are accepted as part of Norman's life.

I must seem in the grip of madness as well, since I'm doing this too. "What does your girlfriend think of the trip?" she asks. This feels like a trick question. Norman looks curious as well. Normally I would say she's working and leading her busy life in New York. Instead I get to the point: "Well, she tolerates it," I say, "or accepts it anyway." I realize I don't know. When you've been together for years it can be hard to tell when charming eccentricity crosses over into low-grade annoyance. Like finding out she doesn't appreciate your favorite tweed jacket. *I thought you liked this!* you protest. *I never said that. I just said it was interesting.*

I look for some sign about how Norman handles this. They both smile, their faces betray nothing. Norman rolls cigarettes in honey-colored paper. I've never seen such healthy-looking cigarettes. Norman is compact, but possesses a vital energy. He has strong eyebrows and engaging dark eyes. His parents live in Patagonia, where he goes each year to wade his favorite river and fish dry flies. I hesitate to tell him I caught a large trout on that river, but on a nymph.

Norman has the charisma of a theater director, an intensity that's directed inward, and an easy smile directed outward. His first language is Italian. His Spanish is accented and his English excellent: self-aware, clear, expressive. "I am so many places at once," he says. "It takes time to get wherever I am." He moves quickly, espresso and cigarettes central to the equation.

After dinner, I walk home through the Gothic Quarter, past young people smoking joints outside bars. Their night is just beginning. I have the strange feeling of being invisible to them. These young people (even using the phrase "young people" is a sign of age) heading out, anything possible, is a feeling I haven't had in a long time. Is this sense of possibility something I try to recreate in fishing? That can't be true, can it?

When Norman picks me up in the morning people are still on the street from the night before. Good grief. Our car is packed with duffel bags, coolers, many rods, wading boots, a few mysterious boxes. This part of a trip is always exciting. There's a coffeemaker with a burner, yes, we might need this. A tarp, a flask, some dried sausage, a knife. You never know.

"I hope this trip we can fish like children," Norman says. We ease out of the city, leave the outer ring of Barcelona, and the buildings fade away. In foreign cities, I'm always surprised when the edge of town begins. I don't expect the countryside to be this close to Barcelona. But here it is and now we start driving up. The mountains are gentle and green and welcoming, with deep valleys. The eastern side of the Pyrenees is Basque. "Basque trout are strong," Norman says and smiles. "Because they're Basque."

Our trip is divided in three sections. In each area we'll fish with one of Norman's friends. More Spanish anglers, an object of curiosity to me. Fishing with somebody new leads to a natural moment of assessment, like setting toddlers down in a sandbox. Sometimes you get a hint of somebody's expertise by certain things they say and how well used their rods and reels are. But of course you really have to see them fish. No use trying to convince anybody that you know what's what by speaking in jargon or showing off an expensive rig. Those people think their Leica makes them Ansel Adams.

And forget about impressing a guide. I understand the urge. But it won't work. Guides don't want to be impressed. There's nothing you can do that they can't do better. The first thing they decide is how tolerable you're going to be over the next seven hours. Then they'll watch you cast and manage line and make a clear-eyed judgment about your skills and what you can reasonably accomplish. This will take about thirty seconds.

On our first stop we're fishing with Miguel, a young

man and yes, a guide, who works in a fly shop. As a guest I'm the one who's assessed. I'm careful not to misrepresent myself. I try to be relaxed and admit when I make a mistake, while not doing anything that interferes with the good feeling of the group. Be on time, stay positive, avoid trees, keep your fly in the water.

Now, since Miguel is a guide, his baseline level of competence will be high. As for Norman, there are clues that he's serious. He collects specific slow-action rods and old Hardy reels that you wouldn't have unless you're up to something. He even has a special fiberglass rod that you don't acquire unless you're at the far range of the angling spectrum. Like seeing somebody's kitchen setup, sometimes you can tell. I'm not worried—I've fished with obsessives before. But I'm starting to get a feeling that there's fanaticism hidden beneath their genial nature.

We pull next to a low-running river, the Cardós, beneath a lovely arched bridge. There's a path people walk and bike down. The river appeals to the locals more as scenery rather than to fish in. That's fine with us. It's early fall and the water is down and very clear. The trout have seen a lot of flies in the summer, so they're educated. Norman and Miguel reiterate this but I'm not worried. After salmon fishing, how hard can these little Mediterranean trout be? We're going to fish like children.

We set up our rods. "What kind of fly line are you using?" Miguel asks, politely. I tell him. "Yes, but which model?" I've forgotten. Maybe I never knew. I like the way the line casts and I don't get caught up in the latest double taper. Like adding a pinch of salt to a recipe. Just relax and cast.

"And how long is your leader?" They use long leaders here. "Nine feet," I say. Silence. Twelve feet, I propose. "Maybe longer," Miguel suggests. "I'm using sixteen feet," Norman adds. Hmmm. A sixteen-foot leader. Now this is concerning. A long leader means the fish are spooky. What size tippet? I ask. Tippet is the fine material—it resembles the strand of a spider's web—that runs from the thicker leader down to the fly. Tippet is what gets tangled in knots and breaks off on large fish. The size of tippet reflects the proportions of the fly and the clarity of the water. 3x or 4x are fairly standard on larger rivers. But I fear the answer here with small flies in flawlessly clear water. So, again, what's the tippet? "6x." They say it in unison. Oh dear. This is going to be technical.

"Actually, I build specific leaders for these streams," Norman says helpfully. His leader, he explains, has a short, thick section then gets lighter suddenly—normally a leader's size descends gradually. He casts in a precise, abrupt motion that shoots the back end of the leader out, then it unfurls and lands gracefully on the water. To arrive at this point—building a specific leader, adjusting your casting motion—does not come by accident. It takes time, curiosity, and expertise. Fishing like children this is not. This is fishing with engineers.

Miguel and Norman possess an intimate knowledge of the different tapers and shapes of lines. The fishing here, I now realize, is hard. I think back to Markley wanting *not exactly the right thing* in Patagonia and how I thought that was unscientific. To Miguel my approach must seem wildly impressionistic, even naïve. I'm flailing around while they take everything into account.

I've shown up at a cookout ready to throw something on the grill and these two are practicing molecular gastronomy. And, just to reiterate, all this work for the smallest goddamn fish you've ever seen. Now I know who I'm dealing with: I'm dealing with ninjas. I realize how wrong I've been. This is not going to be gazing at a stone bridge dreaming of Goya. I'm not going to be casually casting to little trout then going for cerveza and chorizo and feeling good about myself. Not even close.

I ask Miguel how he approaches this stretch of water. He makes a brief cast, tosses in a casual mend before the fly lands—a wave of a few feet of extra line—so there's no drag and his fly doesn't move unnaturally in the current. He does a half dozen high-level moves in about two seconds. This isn't showing off and it isn't gratuitous. It's evolutionary. This is an expert expression of what it takes to catch these fish. So I do as Miguel does. I lengthen my leader all the way to sixteen feet and down to 6x. But it's hard for me to cast with a long leader. In these close quarters there's less fly line out. Casting the weightless leader is a rarefied maneuver. And to make matters worse my leader is so long I can barely see the tiny fly. I'm not a ninja. I would like to say that I'm a ninja-in-training, but I might not be admitted to the ninja academy. There will be no dojo for me.

We move upstream to a pool under a stone bridge. Miguel is hooking fish regularly. There are rising trout, little dimples in the surface. I get the occasional rise to my fly and quickly lift the rod to set the hook but the fish is never there; I keep missing them. After consulting with Norman I realize I'm not missing them. They're rejecting my fly—the drift is unnatural. They rise to the fly with every intention of taking it, then decide at the last moment that something isn't right.

By the tenth rejection it's clear something more is at stake. I don't mind missing fish. But these fish are *actively* expressing their disapproval of my technique. The little bastards are destroying my confidence. Deep breaths. Nothing focuses the mind like failure. Scarcity and difficulty are intensifying their appeal. After yet another rejection this is no longer charming. This is diabolical.

So that's the game they play. They're going to be hard. They're going to be fast. They're going to be a pain in the ass. Who do these fish think they're dealing with? Guess what? I can be a pain in the ass too. Now, there are temperamental issues and tactical ones. My temperament, when challenged, can be as willful as the next defeated angler's. I'm going to bear down, I will not be made a fool of by a nine-inch trout! I should say, I will *no longer* be made a fool of by a nine-inch trout!

Now the question is one of tactics. I'm trying to do too many things at once. I need to strip down my approach. When there are many rises it's hard to focus on one fish. So I stay with one close trout. A cast won't work if there's any drag. Now I make short casts with a little wave of line thrown in at the end, like Miguel did. This helps the drift and makes the fly's movement appear natural. The setting may be relaxing. The fishing is not. But I feel more precise in my approach.

And after a few shorter casts with my insanely long leader, there's a small rise and I set. I've missed so many before, that when I lift the rod I'm not expecting to feel the fish. But it's there, not a lot of weight, but a connection. I strip it in—no need for the reel here—this is not a fish that's going to fight. A large fish is tired by the time you land it. A little fish still has a lot of energy once it's in.

I kneel in the river and when it stops moving I can see it clearly. My first Mediterranean trout. A sweet silver fish covered in black spots with large dark bands down along its flank. This is why they're sometimes called zebra trout. These bands are most visible from above. A minor miracle. I unhook it and it darts away so quickly. I'm more satisfied than I expect.

"You have to work for these fish," Norman says in an understanding tone. This work had not been mentioned in our previous conversations. We're standing on the bank and he rolls a cigarette. Norman has an artful cast. "I love casting. It's aesthetic," he says. "I'm trying to work toward what I can be. Not what I am." I'm starting to appreciate these native fish. We walk up from the bank and sit outside a café. A group of cyclists is staging between their morning and afternoon rides up the Pyrenees. That puts things in perspective as I order a beer and a tostada. The fishing in the Pyrenees feels correct. Like reaching the hilltop, the struggle is worth the view.

● ● ●

Despite my brief success, when I catch fish here, it's random. The next day there have to be adjustments. I just can't cast a sixteen-foot leader well. I will make accommodations to the Mediterranean trout of the Noguera River. But we will also make accommodations to the angler. To me. So the leader is shortened to ten feet. And their PDX flies are too hard to see. I choose the smallest Parachute Adams I have. This stays upright and drifts well. Since I can see the fly clearly I don't need Doc Holiday's reflexes to set the hook.

Now I make more controlled casts. Everything depends on the fly drifting smoothly for a second or two. A perfectly straight cast will drag and the fish won't like it. As Norman advises, I make an abrupt stop with the forward cast. The fly has to hit the water before the line does. Is this exhausting you? I'm sorry, it was hard for me too. I'm here to relax and find myself learning new techniques. But it becomes natural. "You're fishing better than yesterday," Miguel says. Approval from a ninja who's twenty years younger than I am. I say thank you and try not to beam.

We spend the night in the Santuari de Montgarri, an old hotel in the national park. It's charming—there are wooden shelves with ancient hiking shoes and topographical maps on the walls. In the rustic dining room a pair of cross-country skis hangs over the stone fireplace. Dinner is simple and tastes good. Afterward we have a small glass of Kantxa, an herbal digestif served from a green honeycombed bottle.

Next to the hotel is an ancient stone church. The church bells ring everywhere in Spain, even at midnight. Then you awake to bells that hang around the necks of the cows roaming the hills looking for grass. Bells at night. Bells in the morning.

In Spain the fishing and the eating are never far apart, which is a good equation for me. We gather at a tavern before heading out to the water. It's always hard to tell if it's going to be a long commitment. At various times we have tortillas, *bocadilla,* or *huevos rotos,* fried eggs and ham served over potatoes. When there's a sense of urgency, if there's rain in the forecast or we want to fish before a long drive we order coffee, Norman will have a cigarette, and we head out quickly.

One of our headquarters is Meson de la Reina, a low stone building with a family restaurant in back and a rustic café in front. There's a jukebox with such famous Spanish acts as Donna Summer, Pink Floyd, and Spandau Ballet. We drink at the long wooden bar beneath walls covered with black-and-white photos of the area.

Here we meet Alfonso, a policeman, and another angling devotee. Alfonso and Norman do not discuss politics—they agree to disagree. Alfonso is robust, his manner rougher in a jocular way. If a fish rejects his fly he says something in Spanish that Norman explains means *take my balls.* The hand gesture needs no translation.

Alfonso admits to a romantic streak. "As a boy I dreamed of fishing, mountains, woodworking, and Montana." He is curious about the rivers in Montana; he's never been there. He asks questions and I answer in as much detail as he wants to hear. I tell him that the training in Spain will prepare him for success on the Madison, on the Blackfoot, on the spring creeks in Paradise Valley. He smiles broadly.

Alfonso has built two bamboo rods. "I'm a rookie," he protests. The first was for himself; he carefully unwraps it and shows me. Pale yellow, like straw. Impressive. Who was the second for? "My sensei." The man who taught him. We're about to walk down to the Aragón Subordan in the National Park. The river is narrow; there's plenty of perfectly blue water. Alfonso knows every pool. In the morning we split up and fish on our own. I have some success and catch a few small ones. I enjoy these vivid silver fish. They have no slow movements, they dart, like songbirds, beneath the water.

We gather for lunch at the car, dried sausage and beer. Norman makes surprisingly good coffee over a kerosene burner. We take our time, enjoy the mountain sun, and share a quiet contentment.

In the afternoon we fish together and alternate pools. There are large rocks on the bank where you often find fish. The first cast is the best chance. As soon as the fly has drifted through the pool once, they lose interest. "*Todo o nada*," Alfonso says. I appreciate the international angling language. All or nothing. My reflexes are on high alert. If there's a take I set instantly. These fish are so fast. Unfortunately, there is more *nada* than *todo*.

I get into a rhythm, make controlled casts and don't let the fly drift too long. They'll usually take it right away. If you're lucky, you get one or even two. This is a heightened sense of fishing that I'm not used to. I think I'm doing well. If not well at least better. And right now better is good enough for me.

Then I watch Alfonso put on a clinic. Another ninja. He casts farther, with deadly accuracy and incredible line control—his long drifts are perfectly natural, they never drag. It all looks easy—this is his home water, he fishes here all the time. But there's nothing easy about it. There's the theatrical side of a dead-eyed cast, and there's the more invisible skill, just as impressive, of managing a drift so the fly floats naturally down the river in a complicated current.

He catches about five times as many fish as I do, not that anybody's counting. It's a reminder that more fish are caught by the true experts, many more, which is alarming when you apply this ratio to other rivers. All this work for a fish not much larger than a PEZ dispenser. Late in the afternoon Alfonso catches a twelve-inch trout which, under the circumstances, seems huge.

Throughout the national parks are *refugis*—small buildings open to the public where people can escape the weather and even spend the night. Though you wouldn't want to visit some of these when it's dark. In the Embún park, we end our day in the nicest *refugi* we've seen. It was restored and is maintained by a man named Marco, and there are cards pinned to the wall with messages from people thanking him. There's a wooden bar, a fireplace, a table, a few benches. There are illustrations of the local birds and firewood and old newspapers to light it. There's a communal spirit. Alfonso starts the fire. We drink a beer and talk about fishing. We are going to the Irati tomorrow. Alfonso nods. "The Irati is sacred." A man herds his cattle by us on the dirt path. This is the right way to end our time in the mountains.

When I first heard the phrase *technical fishing* years ago it sounded menacing. It still unnerves me. Usually because I don't discover something will be technical until we're on the water. *This was not mentioned on the lodge website!*

Technical fishing requires specific skills acquired over time. In simpler terms: It's hard. There are long downstream drifts on Silver Creek that require patience and nervy sets. Then on DePuy's Spring Creek you have to deal with invisible ant patterns that hurt your eyes as you squint to see them. So you cast close so they're visible. No way, man. You have to put those ants, which look like flecks of dirt, in the far seam along the bank as the sun sets in Paradise Valley. In the end, it adds up to an education.

And Spain is another part of that education. The principles are the same, but this is a new experience, with long delicate leaders and deadly fast takes. What I'm learning in Spain is not a single thing or catching one fish that justifies all the work. This is not salmon fishing. It's a general approach that gets slightly better every hour as I become aware of each part of the process—the cast, the drift, the set. Fighting these fish is fun only in that it represents success, and that it's nice to see their vivid colors up close. What feels good is paying attention to each detail. And it's reassuring to learn something after all these years on the water. I'm not as set in my ways as I feared.

On the nights we're on our own, Norman and I fish until we can no longer see. As the sun sets, the fish become active. You don't realize they're slowing down until it's too late and finally it's dark and the fish stop. Slowly then suddenly, like many things. Then we drive to our hotel and have dinner in a café.

In Spain, I let myself float. I have no expectations. Driving through the countryside, fishing where it looks good, there's no endpoint. It's natural to test yourself on something larger. In this case the test comes against something smaller. The entire enterprise is a study of fine distinctions. Success is never random. The anglers here enjoy the test. I start to love the test too.

We drive down out of the Pyrenees. Being in the mountains for almost a week the scenery becomes routine, one incredible vista after another. You take it for granted even though you shouldn't. The traffic picks up and we see signs for Pamplona. I'm excited to fish the Irati.

Outside another café we meet Paco. Paco is well liked and well known—are all the fishermen in this country friends? We head inside the café, which has bad décor and good food. People keep showing up and joining our table. They're an informal angling club and we'll be fishing together. There's coffee, coarse local wine, which takes some getting used to (and an ice cube), fried eggs, ham, brown bread. It's such a production I'm not sure we'll make it to the river.

Paco is thin, smokes heavily, and laughs easily. He can tie a fly out of any material—even a doll's hair. I'm struck by the image of Paco scouring toy stores and looking at dolls and a clerk asking if it's for a grandchild and Paco saying, *No, the doll is for me. I want the hair to make a fly.* Send us your eccentric visionaries, we will make anglers out of them!

A man comes up to our table who's friendly with the group. He hears we're heading to the Irati and laughs and says something that translates to *Poor the river.* The fish should watch out if Paco's heading there. He laughs again. *Poor the river.* Paco gives Norman and me gorgeous flies he's tied himself in a clever box that he also made, that folds over elegantly and looks almost Japanese. I'm touched. Norman and I agree that these flies are too nice to use. We're a long way from Jake's worms in *The Sun Also Rises.*

The group talks quickly in Spanish. Paco tells a story and they all laugh. Norman turns to me: "Paco doesn't know how to swim." Another man says, "When we wade a deep river he grabs me like a claw." Norman and I follow this merry band down to the Irati. This isn't like the mountains; we park on a quiet highway and walk through a field of dried grass whose season is behind it. I'm eager to see the Irati. Paco warns that the fishing is tough. It's windy today and nobody thinks there will be a hatch.

Even with the harsh conditions we should have a chance at some good fish. After the mountain streams, I've almost forgotten what a large trout looks like. There's something romantic about returning to a river in Europe where Americans fished one hundred years before. On my second cast, to my astonishment, I get a strike on a lovely stream-lined nymph that Paco has tied. I haven't felt a weight like this since I've been in Spain. Before I can say, I thought the fishing was supposed to be hard, the trout has spit out the nymph. I have a feeling that might have been it. Missing an early opportunity can mean a long day.

And it turns out to be one of those tough days. Everybody can see that. The sky is hostile, the wind blows. This is less technical fishing than in the mountains. Everything feels larger here. The river is wider, the trout are bigger. To my surprise, I miss the intimacy of the small streams. Am I threatening to become an angling Buddhist? Will I start boring friends about wild trout on clear streams? Will I turn my back on the brown trout of Patagonia?

After a futile hour, the Spaniards suggest we leave and go for a drink. "Let's stay," I protest. This is my only chance. I want more time. I know the odds are against us but I don't want it to end.

There were hard days for Hemingway too. Years after *The Sun Also Rises*, he returned and the conditions on the Irati disappointed him. He wrote letters about trees cut down for timber, the water warming up, and the trout no longer there.

I resolve to come earlier in the season and do this correctly. Sometimes you fish when you can and have to be happy with that. The fish that I lost was my only action of the day. "Well at least I saw where Hemingway fished." It's nice to imagine them here.

We walk back to the car. Norman looks ahead. "I think they were actually about thirty kilometers further north."

I'm back in Madrid before I fly to New York. I drink a glass of sherry in an old bar with darkened walls. The bartenders look like handsome art students and don't accept tips. I have another sherry and think about the mountain streams. The blue water, the green mountainsides, the technical demands. I think about my friends who love working so, so hard to catch small trout. I appreciate a wild fish that feels true to its water. I can't become a precision angler, can I?

Sometimes you know you're in the right place. Fishing in the mountains was wonderful. It was without the pressure of seeking the final result, of catching a single fish. The experience remained demanding and completely absorbing, and, once I became accustomed to the rhythms, relaxing. I consider clarifying my approach—more control on the water but also fewer distractions off it. A junior ninja with just enough choices.

In the morning I pass through the handsome city and arrive at the airport. The woman at security asks me questions in halting English. She points at my canvas case and raises an eyebrow. "What is this?" She sounds stern. "They're fishing rods," I tell her. "I was fishing in Spain." Her face brightens. "Oohhhhhh," she smiles. "You love to fish?" she asks brightly. I'm not expecting this sweet direct ness, so humane for a security line.

"Yes," I start to laugh. "I love to fish."

CHAPTER VI

SCOTLAND

Last Chance Saloon

When I returned from Norway, my friends took the news about the salmon calamity in stride. In fact, the range of emotions turned out to be quite narrow. *That's too bad,* they said, upon hearing of my heartbreak, and that was that. People who don't fish just want the broad strokes of your trip. *Other than the fishing, was Norway nice?* I wasn't sure how to answer that. Norway was beautiful, of course, the people were lovely. It's a great country and I hope to return. It was too embarrassing to explain that wasn't the point.

Yes, the people had moved on. But one person had not. Not this person. Not me. I remained a lone, brave holdout. I tried to laugh at what I now called the "Norway Situation." I consider myself an aficionado of tales of fishing woe. Bring me your sad stories, I will lend a sympathetic ear. Fishing and loss are never far apart, failure being closer at hand than success. That's why most anglers, however enthusiastic, are familiar with the wistfulness inherent to the sport. Fish a lot and you will lose fish. Hopefully you build enough scar tissue to limit the damage. It can be hard out there.

The best way to get over this, as with a broken heart, is time. The other is by fishing. After Spain, I caught some lovely trout in the Catskills and matters returned to more earthbound proportions. No, I didn't catch a salmon in Norway. That's happened to many people before me. I could laugh, with a hint of pain, at the intensity of Johan's guidance and the things he taught me. I also remembered the landscape, the wondrous rivers, and, the slightly less majestic summer aquavit. After a while these peaceful thoughts weren't enough. I still wanted a salmon.

The most comical issue was that I still wasn't sure I was a good caster. Well, I knew I wasn't good, but I didn't know if I was acceptable. Being acceptable can get you through enough doors, angling or otherwise, and a confident delivery can get you the rest of the way.

Something larger was happening: I was suffering a

salmon emergency. I was not in possession of wisdom, the long view, or a poetic approach to the vagaries of life. I felt desperate. Perhaps Norway hadn't taught me anything except that I wanted to catch a salmon. But I knew that before I went to Norway! Now it was September and this salmon issue had to be resolved, for the fish would stop running up the rivers soon.

This trip wasn't part of the year's master plan. It had to be added to the agenda. It was not a dignified moment when I heard myself saying to a loved one, "I'm going to Scotland. I need to catch a salmon." If this happens to you, then I imagine you'll receive the same blank look that I did.

I needed professional help that only a salmon angler could provide. Ruaridh, from his home in Havana, served as my analyst and spiritual advisor. He viewed my predicament with the sympathy specific to salmon devotees, who have suffered extensively themselves. Ruaridh knew salmon can take over your life. He wanted me to succeed and I appreciated that.

Where can I catch a salmon in Scotland in the next two weeks? I texted, recklessly. Sometimes you can't hide your desperation. Ruaridh had waited his whole life to answer this question. This was too important for text, so I called him. He stepped out onto his balcony and I could hear his baby in the background. He discussed his homeland in great detail. "The River Tweed doesn't have their famous fall run anymore," Ruaridh warned. "But there are other options." I was ready for anything. Some smaller rivers, he suggested, still held fish at this time of year.

"Now, these fish will not be silver," Ruaridh cautioned.

"Does that matter?"

"Well it matters to some of the snobs, who like salmon right from the sea. Chromers, they call them."

He made it sound like, knowing my character, I would align with the snobs.

"The fish now will be darker, but still lovely."

"That's fine with me. But even if they're not silver, do they still count?"

He laughed. "Oh, they count."

Ruaridh connected me with guides who could help. You don't just show up in Scotland and head to the river to fish. Each beat is spoken for and has to be rented for the day, and the better ones by the week. I stared endlessly at a website where I could reserve beats and, crucially, see how productive those beats had been month by month for the last decade or more.

Many salmon trips are booked a year in advance. You meet your friends with a bottle of Scotch and hope the fish are running and that nobody had to get a knee replaced at the last minute. Otherwise you're out of luck. There are no refunds in salmon fishing. If you live in England, you can be more responsive and follow the fish. But most salmon trips aren't that nimble. If this was going to happen, it had to come together fast. Even then nothing would be guaranteed.

After a flurry of reserving beats, guides, hotels, and a car, I fly to Edinburgh in a seat that doesn't recline. The airline website advised me that the seat had "minimum to no recline." Well the difference between these positions turns out to be quite large. After boarding I pressed the button on the armrest and tried to push back, and, drumroll, nothing. Not just a no, but a firm no at that. I sit bolt upright over the Atlantic and hope this is not a bad omen.

This is no time for self-pity, that's already waiting for you on the river. I resolve to stay positive. I get on a train from Edinburgh, a little stiff, but in one piece. Mungo, who's arranged this leg of the trip, gathers me from a train station in Perth and we drive an hour to his uncle Frank's house in the Highlands, not far from Inverness. I feel I have to ask the obvious question.

"What's Mungo a nickname for?"

"Oh, Mungo is my given name."

"Really?"

"Yes, Mungo is the patron saint of Glasgow."

"Oh, I didn't know."

"Yes, I've met a few Mungos before. But usually they're cats or dogs. I'm one of the few Mungos who can speak."

To be clear, Mungo is not burly or imposing. He manages estates throughout Scotland, letting them to hunting and fishing parties. He's fished many rivers and knows the country homes and their owners. He guides occasionally and I'm lucky that he will guide me. He's at ease around men, many well-heeled, who want to stalk a stag or catch a salmon. He's young and appealing and has no noticeable accent. He's immediate and unaffected. I like him at once.

Mungo's uncle Frank has rights to fish a small river called the Farrar, which flows into the larger and more well-known Beauly. The Farrar winds through a scenic valley and on the far bluff are Scottish pines that can be centuries old. There is an upstream dam that is not centuries old. It was built after World War II when power generation was the government's priority. The dam is out of sight from where we fish but a fact of modern life in this ancient place. One benefit of fishing a tailwater like this is that the dam guarantees a water level that would welcome migrating salmon this late in the year.

We get closer to Inverness in the early afternoon. "We could go straight to the river," Mungo says. "And fish right now." This feels like a pivotal moment in our early friendship. Am I going to return to the guesthouse, settle in, and relax after an upright overnight flight? Or am I going to go straight from the plane to the train to the car to the river to the salmon? There's only one choice.

"Let's fish."

"That's a good man."

Before I really consider the momentous nature of what we're undertaking Mungo and I are standing in our waders along the banks of the Farrar. Mungo knows the water well. He hands me his rod and, not to put too fine a point on it, I cast pretty well. That may be overstating things, as I set the bar low. But I am aggressively adequate and feel, despite the jet lag, great. Who doesn't love arriving in Scotland?

"You're doing fine," Mungo says. "Now keep casting the same distance and let it swing through those riffles." We have an hour of daylight left and then we're set to meet friends, including Matt, who's stag hunting on the same estate. Mungo believes this is a good time for fishing. I think of salmon as something you need to devote days to, not catch easily right when you arrive in town. "The fish won't be silver," he warns me, as did Ruaridh. I don't care. Any Atlantic salmon will do.

There's a lot of discussion about what to do when a salmon actually takes. This is considered in great detail because there's so much time when you're not catching anything that you fill it with analysis about what to do when you finally catch one. Like deciding how you'll spend your money when you win the lottery. It's nice to dream before ripping your useless ticket in half.

When a salmon takes a fly, it returns to where it was holding, usually without being aware of the hook. Some people believe you should let the fish set itself. That's to say: Let the fish move until you feel a weight and then, once it starts to turn, raise the rod. Many of my fellow tragic trout anglers feel a tug and, as they've been conditioned to do, raise the rod. *Noooooo!* This is a terrible turn of events. The fly will be removed from the salmon's mouth, sailing through the air, failure made tangible, while the salmon remains underwater, where it will not be caught again.

If, blessings on us all, there is a slow, sustained tug, that's a fish. Though how would I know? All my information is secondhand or grilse-related. There will be pressure on the line when the salmon realizes what's going on. The fly we're using is a red shrimp with a double hook that Mungo tied himself, which swings just below the surface. When Mungo and I have been standing in the Farrar about fifteen minutes, I feel the elusive knock. A persistent pull on the line. A salmon. After all this painful speculation from Canada to Norway to Scotland, I'm not sure I'm in the zone to deal with a salmon.

I keep the rod pointing at the water, doing what I'm supposed to be doing, letting the fish return to its lie and set itself. I begin to float into the realm of unreality. This is my time. I have visions of greatness. I'm going to get a tattoo of the Scottish flag on my shoulder. I'm going to name my dog Mungo. I going to rent a room from Frank, move in, and become an honorary Highlander.

Finally Mungo turns to me. "Raise the rod," he says with some urgency. I promptly do that. And feel a quick, sharp resistance. Then nothing. No fish. My mouth moves but no sounds come out. I just had a salmon. And I botched it. Gentle laugh from Mungo. "You have to raise the rod," he says, as if I expected to enter a foreign country without a passport. "You have to set the hook." "I thought the fish set itself," I protest, desperately. This is a reminder in every angling situation to ask what you should do in the event of a strike.

I'm not prepared for success, so shell-shocked am I from Norway. I honestly didn't expect to catch a fish quickly. It's a classic mistake—there's no predictable rhythm to being on the water. The fish can arrive when they're not supposed to be there. Being aware at all times is inherently difficult. But not believing something can happen is far worse. Norway was a washout. So, intuitively, Scotland would be too. Mungo even said, "I think we have a chance at one today." I dismissed that as friendly optimism to raise morale. Ugh.

When you lose a fish in front of somebody, you want to justify your error. Your mistake should be based on a well-researched fallacy—so get other people involved. Well I was fishing with a friend and he referred to an article that a guide gave him that offered advice that I was following. What the hell? Live in the moment, man! Nobody cares what you thought you were trying to do that backfired spectacularly. Just raise the damn rod.

Whatever else this episode proves, we know there are fish in the river. And they're active. We see another salmon jump, a burst of gray a hundred yards downstream. All right. This is going to happen. Or this could happen. Let's not get ahead of ourselves. But the sun goes down and nothing more happens today. I head to the hotel, where I meet with Matt. He shot a stag so he's happy. I'm in that state beyond jet lag where tiredness and excitement reach an uneasy truce. We eat good lamb in Inverness and have a nightcap of a Scotch I've never heard of, which, not surprisingly, is incredible.

The next morning, Mungo and I are ready for success. There's frost on the late-season grass, but the sun suggests it will warm quickly. We stop at Frank's farmhouse while terriers run around our heels. Frank, a kind-eyed, genial man looks great in well-worn estate tweed. He's generous with tea prepared on a red AGA stove. "I think the conditions are good," Frank assures me. Mungo agrees. I'm not sure how to deal with these positive assessments. I can't tell if they just want to send salmon anglers off to war with a cup of tea and a smile on their face.

The Farrar is a winding river, often reached climbing

down hills. We fish pools that require a hand-drawn map to find. Once one has arrived there's more to do. Are the fish at the top of the pool? At the bottom? We fish a remote pool. Nothing. But it's lovely and feels good as the sun comes out in Scotland. Clouds arrive suddenly; there's no way to get used to the weather. Everybody in Scotland is aware of the elements and at their mercy. In the distance we hear guttural roars of rutting stags, looking for mates.

Late in the morning we head to a pool near the road. There's a bench in front of the water, usually the sign of a good run. And it did used to be great, apparently. All the records are kept. Frank shows me an album with black-and-white photos of previous generations standing in the pools, smiling at the camera. There are carefully recorded results of salmon caught in each beat—*The Long Pool, 2; The Gorge, 7*—from every month going back decades.

I will never get used to salmon rivers. They would calm anybody; yet I feel some nerves. I cast my shrimp and let it swing. Every cast or two I step down and cover more water. The Farrar feels manageable. And with Mungo I feel a level of assurance

A few casts later I feel a knock. A persistent, dead weight, but it's not dead. I know. The line straightens. Mungo knows too. "There," he says. This is a fish. There's the sustained pull. Nothing dramatic. I wait a few beats, and then, as Mungo instructed, I raise the rod. The fish is on. I am connected to a salmon. "Just keep the pressure on," Mungo says. The salmon continues to head upstream and I reel in. This can't be happening. I do actually know how to reel in a fish. I've done it before. I don't know what I'm expecting. I'm trying to assess the experience when suddenly the salmon jumps—the size of my arm—then stiffly falls in the water. That's a salmon all right. This is no longer an abstraction. That jumps brings our worlds together. I try not to act shocked, but I'm awestruck.

Mungo moves below me with his net. I back up on the bank. Everything is steady. And not completely unlike fighting a steelhead or even a large trout. But this is a salmon. An Atlantic salmon! The space of speculation has been filled in with fact. And, strangely, this feels natural. I want to land the fish but I don't want this to end. I know that on some level no fish will ever be the same.

Mungo is calm and his competence is contagious. "Just keep it coming," he says. There's no last dash from the fish. Nothing evil happens. The angling gods don't get devilish. I lift the rod and Mungo makes a smooth maneuver with the net, which now holds a salmon. "There you go," Mungo says, grinning. I start laughing. "Oh my god!" Nothing more articulate than that. Just a shout of joy. I say it was never in doubt when it was only ever in doubt. I'm ecstatic, relieved, and embarrassed I cared so much in the first place.

The color is dark silver with a deep pink band down its middle. Slate-gray with small black spots spread apart a good distance from each other. Mungo kneels in the river and holds the tail of the salmon as it begins to regain energy in the shallow water. Ten pounds, Mungo says, though it may have been eight. Whatever the number: It counts.

Frank is happy when we tell him. He may feel a sense of pride that he's the steward of a wonderful river. In this part of the world word spreads about a salmon. Somehow people in the hotel know, friends know. *Heard you had a good day on the river*, they say. The Farrar will always have a place in my heart. It's really true, you never forget the first time.

I drive from Edinburgh toward the River Tweed. There's a farcical situation trying to rent a car—they don't have the small car I reserved. In the name of an upgrade, they install me behind the wheel of an immense Mercedes. I will be driving this silver behemoth on narrow, winding roads lined with hedges and stone walls. No easy trick. The interior trim is illuminated with purple lights. This is not the car for a pastoral angling retreat. This is the car for a nightclub owner.

I do not want to scratch this car I didn't ask for. So driving requires more concentration than fishing. I make it to the border between England and Scotland. I feel like a fool as I move slowly down the high streets of market towns. I stay in a hotel on the edge of a village where people come to fish. There's an airy pub with a good restaurant—I have delightful sole fillets for dinner. The pub is full of anglers and ghillies still in their clothes from the water. There are old maps of the River Tweed on the wall. This is where it's done.

In the morning I drive to Bemersyde, a well-known beat on the Tweed. I meet Finlay, my guide. Fin and I have been in touch over the previous week and we worried there wouldn't be enough water to fish. In classic Scottish tradition, so much rain fell over the weekend that now there's too much water to fish. That's that. There will be no fishing. Thanks for coming, have a nice day.

Thankfully Fin has his own beat farther up the Tweed. We can fish there despite the long odds. Fin is tall and thin and low-key, agreeable and not like most guides I've met. Like a genial clerk at a record store (in fact, he played in a band in Edinburgh). For lunch he brings pork pies from a local butcher and dark chocolate. We eat well and he's good company. We don't catch anything.

The next day we are on Glenmoriston beat. The beats are named after landowners, long deceased, geographic features, or just nicknames. Since this is Scotland some, on first glance, are hard to pronounce to the outsider: Ashiestiel, Traquair, Dawyck. We meet at the hut and the ghillie is young and kind, not what I expected. He tells Fin where we'll fish in the morning, we'll fish a different beat in the afternoon. Another ghillie emerges from the hut with strong, sweet tea with milk. In the situation it tastes great. There are horses in the fields beside the river. They belong to the owner, an Irishman who's crazy about horses. Doesn't love anglers.

Guides and ghillies are aware of the diminishing numbers of salmon. Naturally their jobs depend on anglers and their success. But it's not just self-interest. Everybody here has fished for decades. They have watched the runs reduce or end completely. There's an underlying sadness, like a cold fall breeze when winter is coming.

The Tweed here is not as broad as it is down in the famous beats. Salmon that arrive here have passed more anglers. Fin asks where I've been fishing and I tell him about my Farrar success. He's probably relieved that I'm not counting on catching a fish with him. We're playing with house money.

I cast and swing and have a fish on. Fin is not for lifting the rod when there's a take. Keep the rod tucked between your body and your elbow to keep from raising it. As the fish comes into view, it's our friend, the grilse. I reel in until this grilse is opposite me, fifteen feet from the bank. Then ten feet. We see it clearly. "Five pounds," Fin says. I keep reeling and the fish shakes off. Fin takes this development harder than I do. We saw the fish. It wasn't an adult salmon. And it stays in the water. What's the difference for the last few feet? "Might want to be a little more patient when you're reeling," Fin says, as politely as possible.

The disappointment intensifies back at the hut. Walter, the ghillie, asks Fin how we did.

"Well, we lost one."

"Oh I see."

"What?" The assistant ghillie asks as he comes out of the hut.

"He lost one."

"Who?"

"Him. The American."

"Lost one?"

"Yes, a grilse."

"Oh too bad."

"And he hooked another," Fin adds. I may have forgotten to mention that brief connection.

"What?"

"He lost one and hooked another. Didn't land either."

"So no fish?"

"No. None."

This is an extensive discussion about fish I lost. It's not exactly how I would have recounted the situation. I try to interject "Well, it was a grilse." I don't want to sound defensive but I want to make a clean account of what happened. I would also add that we fought it to the bank and, it was within a rod's length, and that counts for me. But not for the beat. The lost grilse can't go into the log. It's not official. As far as Fin, the ghillies, the River Tweed, and the country of Scotland are concerned, there was no fish. All that remains is a sense of communal regret aimed in my direction.

I am now aware that any fish I become involved with has repercussions beyond myself. I promise Fin that I will be patient with any fish, even a grilse. I promise I will not raise my rod. The river has fish in it—that's the important fact. After lunch I'm eager to get back on the bank. Fin is confident too, but doesn't say much.

We head to our new beat and I quickly feel a knock. I wait. I don't raise the rod, I do it Fin's way (sorry Mungo). The fish is on. Patience and pressure. No jump. I am catching salmon, albeit of modest size; Fin nets a ten-pounder, with the hooked lower jaw. A male. A dark fish. Gray with the faintest streak of pink. A handful of black spots. Fin keeps the fish in the water as he slips the hook from its mouth. He holds it upright. It does not swim away but holds in the shallows. We stare at the black back until, finally, it moves upstream.

I am a new man. I am a catcher of salmon, a veteran, you

might say. This is official. This counts toward the numbers. This is fun and not that fraught. Is there enough requisite suffering here? I'm not sure I can understand salmon fishing as a simply enjoyable afternoon.

We're in a festive mood, like a blackjack table where the dealer busts. Fin heads back to the hut for another leader. He asks if I'll be all right on my own for five minutes. With my newfound confidence I think I can handle matters. "Just back up and pull the fish onto the bank, right?" I say breezily. I mean what could be easier? "That's it," he says.

Once Fin is over the slope and out of sight I have a knock. *Stay calm.* This is unreal. I'm alone with a salmon on the line. Another test. What's the worst that could happen? I keep pressure on. The salmon swims upstream, but stays in the middle of the river. It does not approach the bank. There's an amazing moment the first time the fish is visible. I see the salmon, a flash of silver beneath the current reflecting in the sunlight. Not bright silver, but still vivid, lined with pale pink.

Swimming against the current is tiring. After a few minutes there's less pressure. I'll have to back up and pull the fish onto the bank. The salmon is opposite me, in shallow water. I try to be clinical. It's time for me to move.

I back up. The fish is in a few inches of water. I hear Johan's words, *When the fish is on the bank you have thirty seconds.* The fish seems tired but relaxed. *You have thirty seconds.* Setting the rod down is hard to do. It goes against every fishing instinct; we are told to keep the pressure on. Here there will be no pressure. I point the rod away from the river so I won't step on it. Another fear of mine. Losing a fish *while* breaking a rod—the exacta from hell.

The rod is on the ground. Miraculously, the salmon stays where it is. There's no tension on the fish. Theoretically it could swim away and I would have to go get the rod. But it remains still. I head down to the water. I approach from behind, staying out of its line of vision. I reach down and in one move grip the band above its tail. I tighten my left hand. That part of the fish is firm. It's a clean take.

I put my other hand under her stomach and ease the salmon upright into deeper water. Up close the stripe is the gentlest rose. How far has this salmon voyaged out into the world? Today she and I are together in the River Tweed. I move her slowly in the water and she revives. Miraculously, the fly, an Ally's Shrimp, falls easily from her mouth. Who can say about these things? A twelve-pound hen. A salmon landed on my own. The ideal. The salmon sits in the shallows and I watch until she swims away. I'm overwhelmed with affection for the Tweed and the fish that return here from the Atlantic. I feel weightless as I stand next to the river and wait for Fin to come back, to tell him the good news.

Now Johan is correct about one thing: It's incredibly satisfying to catch a salmon, or any fish, on your own. The sense of accomplishment, certainly, but also the self-contained nature of solitary action in a large space. This drama played out according to plan. You look around and nobody's

THE BELIEVER

there. It's a secret, unknown to all but you. That rare private moment is why we return to the water.

There's also the physicality, the sensation of fighting
and landing a fish. A mixture of adrenaline and nerves and
self-control. And then the fight is over and the rightness
of the world without our impression upon it returns. Our
intrusion is brief, as it should be. We remain out of our element. We never know what happens beneath the surface.
Even when the water is clear, all we know is the impressions of things. And a few triumphs that are more than we
deserve and never enough.

When we fish we imitate and disappear. Reflect what the
fish eats and hide any trace of ourselves. We get closer to
the natural world by trying to mirror cycles of life that have
existed long before we have. Fishing is practiced and technical, yet out of our control, an act of submission. Not to a
higher power, but to the complexity of the natural world,
where animals live, beside us. When I fish I feel leveled,
penitent.

Finally I head back to the hut. I say goodbye to Fin and the
ghillies and their dogs and put my waders and boots into
the back of the Mercedes, gleaming next to mud-covered
Defenders. I pull out onto the dirt track that turns into a
paved pathway where people walk along the river.

The rare day of days. I'm enjoying the afterglow that
was a long time coming. I settled my account. On the
track along the river I drive as slowly as a car will go, and
see more people than I remember. They look annoyed—

do they not like German cars? They glare with thinly controlled anger. Do they not care about my salmon triumph? They get their dogs out of the way and pull their children close as I inch by. The road is longer than I remember and grows narrower and narrower. Hedges close in along with the occasional gatepost. A moment ago I was basking in my success and enjoying the evening light. Now I have to concentrate on navigating this enormous car.

Something is wrong. I don't remember this wall. These trees aren't the same. I've missed the turn and reach a dead end. There's no way to get out other than reversing back down the narrow lane in the silver behemoth. A gray-haired man I saw in an apple orchard that afternoon, approaches the car. I'm afraid he's going to yell at me. "I'm so sorry," I say. And add redundantly: "I missed the turn." "Yes," he exhales, calmly, as if addressing an errant schoolboy. "You're in a bit of a pickle."

There are hedges on both sides of the car. I start to back up. There's a video on my dash of the road behind me but it's grainy and doesn't help. Some beeper has been going off constantly as I brush against various branches. The man walks beside the car, kindly guiding me. "Keep coming," he says. "Keep coming." I'm dreading getting an enormous scratch along the door of this car I didn't ask for. Then dealing with the rental place. Charges. Disputes. Does Mungo know a small claims lawyer?

We pass all the people I drove by minutes ago. Then I was driving forward. Now I'm driving backward. This is not something you experience unless you're Jacques Tati.

175

They must have known this was going to happen and were waiting for me to realize my mistake. Now, inevitably, we meet again. "Sorry!" I yell through the open window. "This is not my car." My angling triumph feels too short-lived.

Then my conductor says, "You can back up here." There's a small opening in the hedge and I put the car in reverse and ease up onto a matted pile of brush. The car is absolutely shrieking with technological unhappiness. I move inch by inch. "Don't be shy!" he exclaims and seems to be enjoying this wayward expedition. I'm grateful for his help. I finally spin around in an excruciating eight-point turn and am back on the path in the right direction. This time I make the turn—man, I went a long way by it—and breathe easily. I think about a day where it all came together and wonder why I never believed something this good could ever happen.

CHAPTER VII

AMERICA

Fishing the States

The year was winding down and it was time to focus closer to home. No airports, no forty-pound bags, no jet lag. Honestly, it was a relief. I'm not sure it's natural to fish this much. Wise souls will say that should be obvious, one or two *did* say that. Quite directly in fact.

I know people who are on the water a hundred days

a year, more. Once you enter this world you meet obsessives who've made fishing the operating principle of their lives. The calendar of fish they pursue becomes their calendar. That's the risk knowing the devotees—you start to think their behavior is normal. You justify a trip by saying it's not that long, that *Peter's going to Patagonia for two months.* The response: *What does Peter have to do with this?*

Back in New York it was good to be in our apartment and eat dinner for two. Everything seemed to have gone on well enough without me, it wasn't clear I was really missed, which I suppose was a good thing. I didn't know where to fish. I just knew wherever it was I would drive there. Laying out a fishing trip can take forever, or it can come together quickly, when a car's involved. You're nimble and can respond to the facts on the ground. When I drive my car, the illustrious Swedish fishing mobile, there's the reassurance that comes with having *Everything I Could Possibly Need.* This is a dynamic collection that I add to and subtract from, trying to find the right balance.

We start with an array of fishing rods, reels, fly boxes, waders, boots, backup waders and boots. These waders are rolled up in the wagon's designated "Wet Section," a large cardboard box that was once a beer case, back when cases were sturdy because you returned the empty bottles to receive your deposit. But usually you just exchanged the empties and bought another case so the cycle continued into beer infinity. They don't make cases that way anymore, which is too bad. The box also holds boots, a rain jacket or two, and anything that's been in water.

There are other sections in other boxes: "Cooking/

Dining": a variety of knives, brown enamel plates, one of those Italian coffeemakers, an AeroPress (which makes better coffee but is less romantic), a cork cutting board, which turns out to be surprisingly useful. "The Library": an Evelyn Waugh novel I bought on the road, a few of the Roderick Haig-Brown books I buy whenever I find them, red-covered gazetteers of detailed maps of Montana and Idaho and Wisconsin that are now mostly irrelevant in the digital age, that I keep anyway. There are cigar boxes full of cards of local fly shops, a screwdriver, and an oyster knife I got in New Brunswick and used once, miraculously with no loss of blood.

There are various duffel bags, khaki or olive canvas, devoted to shirts, sweaters, and chinos, another full of jackets. A third for towels, shorts, bandanas, there might be some napkins. A swimsuit and shorts, a tartan scarf somebody brought back from Scotland, a parka. You may laugh but if you need a raincoat then you'll admire my diabolical foresight.

In the car are more necessities: a lighter, a bottle opener, some good Japanese toothpicks (once you've used them you can't go back), a waterproof watch, a tin of Altoids, containers of salt and pepper, truck stop Advil. In the rack along the door there's a case of sunglasses and a Tom Petty CD—this car derives from the last year they were built with compact disc players—there's also R.E.M.'s *Document*, Camper Van Beethoven, and a great Wilco album. Drive around America and listen to American music, man.

This master plan of angling preparation is the result of a boyish impulse that, like many childhood impulses, takes decades to master. Every part of the wagon is arranged according to a combination of science and intuition, like a personal library, that makes sense to me. You're welcome to behold this organizational situation, help yourself to a beer from the cooler (rear left of the trunk). But don't get any ideas about putting your bags back there—it's at maximum capacity. You'll notice that I've cleared out an area behind your seat that should be more than enough for what you've brought.

This wagon replaced a dearly departed Saab that I also drove all over the country. The check engine light had been on longer than any relationship I've ever had, but you stop worrying about that after a year. The turbo engaged reluctantly and finally went on permanent hiatus. Ultimately, I would be overtaken by cars (and some lighter trucks) on any highway with a steady incline. I started dreading the sight of hills.

Finally I had to admit what was what—I couldn't trust the old Saab to drive from New York to Montana—which is really the standard for a car for me: It has to be Swedish, it has to be black, and it has to make it out West. If a car can't get you to Montana, why even have it? In a private moment I finally looked up the Saab's blue book value and the number I found was insulting, even hurtful. It was, apparently, worth less than dinner for two according to these experts who were possibly Norwegian, so clear was their anti-Swedish bias.

I took some time to myself and considered the options. I finally made a measured decision and think I made the right choice: I traded the car for a fishing rod. Oh and a reel too. Don't forget about the reel. I'd told a friend about the Saab situation; he said he didn't mind about a check engine light or the complete lack of acceleration or the mysterious jangling sound, and that he knew a mechanic who could deal with it. He was going to teach his daughter to drive a manual transmission and it seemed like a win all around. How much did I want? Oh no, I said, I couldn't accept any money. The car was like a house with a roof that could collapse at any moment. I didn't want to be blamed when the rain came in. Well, what would be a good trade? We settled on a fishing rod and reel, and that was that. Later, when I asked him about the car, he said it was fine, but I noticed a rueful smile cross his face.

So, the car was packed, the issue was which way to point it. What type of fishing and where? Trying to answer these questions inevitably leads to more questions. Do you want solitude? Do you want action? Do you want familiarity? Novelty? Long odds? Regular success? Maybe you want to see a friend and fish new water. Something you've discussed for ages suddenly comes together and the next thing you know you're driving across a few states.

That's what happened earlier in the summer. I drove from Wisconsin to Wyoming (a trip you can make in a single day, if arranged strategically, armed with a box of Snyder's pretzels). I fished with a friend, Mike, who had told me about some rivers he thought I would like. The timing aligned and suddenly I was heading west on I-94. Modern technology tells you how far to the nearest gas station, where there's a traffic jam, what time you should arrive. Convenient for sure, but the mystery is drained away.

Before, you would estimate when you would make it half-way across the country within an hour or two. Now you know within minutes.

I met Mike in Sheridan, Wyoming, at a famous old bar on Main Street, the wood-paneled walls covered with the requisite taxidermy. There were countless photos, now faded, of anglers standing proudly behind rows of fish laid out on the grass. I always feel uneasy at the sight of these photos, dozens of trout dead in the sun.

There are cold streams in warm places where trout thrive. They seem incongruous, so near the heat of the high plains. Here, a place Mike knew well, the stream flowed dark over stones, gently rolling hills in the distance, the yellow grass cut short. The cows, if they ever came down here, were somewhere else.

Mike is a former guide and an alarmingly good caster. My window for success turned out to be much narrower than his. Quite literally: On the stream where we were fishing, the casting was between overhanging branches. You had a small window to land your hopper close to the bank, to give yourself the best chance to catch aggressive brown trout. But you had to get that cast right up against the bank. These fish were active, but, like New York real estate, the issue was location, location, location. How greedy did you want to be? You could cast your hopper through an opening knowing that if you missed you would get tangled in the branches and lose your rig. Or you could play it safe and cast outside the bushes and hope the fish would come those extra few inches away from their lie.

This is one of the eternal questions. We imperfect cast-ers try to reassure ourselves that inches won't matter, that the fish will come if the fly is, dreaded phrase: close enough. *Au contraire.* Watch somebody who knows what they're doing and you'll see the importance of every inch. You'll find a rising trout that refuses to deviate from its feeding lane. You can go crazy about these things or try to be as accurate as you can. I'd rather miss a fish by doing what I trust, as opposed to sinking matters with an ambitious cast I can rarely pull off.

Mike makes difficult things seem easy, then you think they'll be easy for you, and the next thing you know your line is broken off and you hear yourself saying, *Mike, why don't you give it a shot, while I tie on another hopper.* By the afternoon I thought we'd done well. Mike said the fishing was good, though not as good as it usually was. Isn't that always the way?

The next day we fished on a small river that flowed through a ranch. There was an arrangement that was deadly serious. I was instructed not to share any landmarks that might betray this place to anybody else. So Mike blindfolded me until we parked the car. He didn't, but probably thought about it. There are mercenary anglers out there who keep their secrets from even more mercenary anglers. They post photos in reverse and edit out recognizable bridges and rocks. Nothing can be known. Of course, they could keep the photos to themselves, but they can't help posting their triumphs. Apparently, catching the fish isn't enough.

This was a genial river where trout would be happy to live. Classic dry fly water. But no insects were coming off and no fish were rising. I don't remember whose idea it was to try a black streamer—yes, we were desperate. The second it landed a fish came bolting off the bank to take it. So much for the finer distinctions.

We wondered if this was an accident. It was not. These trout were keyed in on streamers. My lasting memory was catching a trout that I reeled in at what I considered a reasonable clip. When it was five feet away the fish jumped in front of me and was much larger than I realized. I stared in amazement at the huge black back of a brown trout. It ejected the fly and landed in the river, and that was that. It happened so suddenly. In the moment these things are shocking. None of the other fish were that big, I wanted to protest. Well no kidding, what do you think we're doing here? Trying to catch the bigger fish. The same trout Mike's been talking about for years. The same reason you drove all day to get here.

This highlighted one of my less distinguished habits: Impatience. I can fish for a long time and catch nothing— that kind of patience is no problem. And I can drive halfway across the country again, no problem. My better half calls me *Long Distance Dave*, when I happily prepare for twelve hours behind the wheel. But the moment a fish is on the line, I reel in quickly. I want to resolve the situation. I think it's better to fight a fish aggressively. Reeling slowly allows more time for something to go wrong. And you don't want to tire out the fish too much. It's still good to be patient, especially when you don't know how big the fish is. The fish swam toward me so I couldn't feel its size (another excuse, I'm sorry). Now I had to come to terms with this lost fish. I caught a few more but nothing of such impressive proportions. When I made it around the bend to find Mike, he tried not to get too detailed about his success, but he couldn't stop laughing. Which I interpreted as a good sign. Woolly Buggers. "It's not supposed to be like that here," he said. Who knew?

That night we felt lucky enough to gamble on the only Mexican restaurant in town. My margarita came in a glass the size of a goldfish bowl. And the food wasn't bad. It was a fast trip. I drove through South Dakota, and made a quick stop in Wall Drug for a doughnut on the way back to our cabin.

On this lake in Wisconsin is where I learned to fish. Our wood cabin sits on a small hill up from the water. It was built in 1929 by my great-grandfather. There's a stone fireplace that's welcome when summer arrives late or fall arrives early. The lake is deep and clean and I try to swim every day.

The first question people ask is about electricity or running water. I'm sorry to report that it has both. Some can barely hide their disappointment that we're not living in a aggressively rustic setting. I appreciate that your friend's uncle has a place lit only by candles. That's great. I'm sure it's delightful when he takes out his ukulele and strums the evening's entertainment. Nobody is claiming to suffer here. Refrigeration and plumbing and lights are good inventions, in my view.

I should add that the house isn't winterized and there's

heat in only one of the bedrooms and . . . why am I try-ing to prove that it's more demanding than it is? When we were growing up we slept on the "children's porch," which just had screens and could get cold. My sister and I had many strategies to warm our beds, and you didn't move once you established your area of heat. We would tell each other frightening stories about what might be in the woods, in the absolute dark, and fell asleep in exhilarated terror.

The cabin faces west across the lake, which is good for sunsets but not when a storm arrives, and if it's serious we have to lower green canvas blinds over the windows so water doesn't come in. Then the cabin closes in, the wind rattles, and you feel the thrill and vulnerability of remem-bering the world is more powerful than you.

We have an improbable-looking wooden dock that extends far into the lake and is perfect for diving. And it was on this dock, when I was a boy, where I started to fish, the way a child fishes, happily, with few expectations. I love this lake, instinctively, like a sibling, but it has to be said that it's not a great fishing lake. That's not how I judge these things, and I come here whenever I can, but I don't fish here much any more.

When I was young my grandfather didn't fish but he liked the fact that I did. He was a professor at the Uni-versity of Chicago and believed in the power of expertise. If you were going to play chess then you read books on chess, if you were going to play cards you studied *Accord-ing to Hoyle*, and if you were going to fish then you talked to Carter and Dave. These were his friends and legendary anglers. As a boy, they intimidated me and I preferred to

fish on my own. I waited until I was in my twenties, after
my grandfather died, before I had the courage to head out
on river trips with them. I regret that to this day. How different my life would have been if I'd learned from them
sooner. I could have been a contender.

With Carter and Dave fishing became a learning experience but also a shared experience. We were united in a
mission, though that mission was simply trying to catch
smallmouth bass. Sometimes we spoke a lot, sometimes not
at all. Over the years the time on the water adds up. It's not
just the water. It's loading the vans at 6 a.m., driving to the
river, and eating in dive bars after fishing.

For years we set out in Dave's Old Town canoe on small
rivers whose names I still won't reveal, as Dave swore me
to secrecy. Fishing in Wisconsin has become bittersweet.
I haven't gone out since Carter and Dave died a number
of years ago. Without him, fishing didn't feel right. Dave
would have scoffed at this. He was the least sentimental
person I've ever known.

That water was more closely tied to friendships than I
realized. That's true of many things that become clear in ret-
rospect. It was tied to men of an older generation. With Dave
and Carter I heard stories about my grandfather, Walter. As
I got older I liked learning what he was like with his friends.
He seemed so old to me when I was a boy, which embarrasses me now since he was an active man just in his sixties.

Maybe I fear returning to those rivers that remind me of
things that no longer exist. One day I'll head back. I'm sure
Dave and Carter wanted to pass down what they knew to
me. Maybe I need a younger person to share that knowl-

edge with. I still have flies that Dave and Carter tied and I look at them sometimes. Such small things representing so much knowledge.

I'm not sure when I was first struck with the thought about fishing with a young person, of teaching them some of what I know. That signifies something larger, of course, having children, being a father. This came to me late, about when I turned forty. Then the idea just arrived. The desire to teach somebody—especially a relative—how to fish is fraught with peril. My friend Tom knows a psychoanalyst who said never teach anybody to fish who you see naked. Kids, girlfriends, whoever. This may be the best advice on the matter. When you love something, you expect to transfer that affection onto people close to you. And certainly fishing can be kept in the family—many of my friends learned from their fathers—but sometimes the intensity is too much and children go their own way.

When you're young it's hard to see your family clearly from the inside. So many things I learned from my parents seemed natural. A love of literature and art, of travel, a love of our cabin and our life here. Of my grandfather's curiosity and passion for storytelling. I took that inheritance for granted. As I got older I realized how lucky I was.

Our parents introduced my sister and me to their friends—actors, painters, gallery owners, composers, opera singers, costume designers who sewed their own clothes— and even though we were kids we were expected to interact with them. We loved the dinner parties at our house every Monday night—the theater's night off so actors could come. Red wine in Duralex glasses, cigarette smoke, people speaking French, food passed around right from the grill. Then we went off to bed, the party continued downstairs, outside, in many rooms, voices trailing upstairs behind us. That's an education.

At some point you think about what you want to pass on. You have some theories—how to start a fire, that it's important to drive a manual transmission, that you should read *The Catcher in the Rye* even before you understand it. When I'm at my cabin I think about the past and the future. Now smoke arrives from forest fires. I think about the landscape and the water. How we appreciate the natural world and how we protect it, or, presume somebody else will do that for us.

I go down to our dock, practice casting, and let my mind wander. Standing at this height makes it easier to cast well. When I feel pleased with myself I wade into the lake and try the same cast. Those conditions are less forgiving. We all cast beautifully when there are no fish around. When you have one chance at a large trout that's a different equation.

I drive back to New York at the end of the summer, as I do every year. The first time I drove east was three decades ago, out to college in Maine. Heading from the Midwest to the East Coast I still feel a sense of leaving my childhood home as I get closer to New York where I've made my life. I try not to be sentimental about it and I've learned some things in that time. One is to avoid Gary, Indiana, during rush hour.

You can fish for trout in many places you might not expect. We associate trout fishing with the famous rivers out West. There are plenty of trout in mountain streams that locals would rather keep to themselves. Ask somebody from North Carolina about this and they'll say *We don't know what you're talking about.* But they know very well indeed.

There are trout in nearly every state. Tailwaters flow from dams. The air is humid but the water stays cold, and trout like the cold. Some of these tailwaters are in the South. One of the best is the South Holston, in Tennessee.

The South Holston is unknown to many people and well known to fewer people. The people who know keep going because of the possibility of catching a brown trout that they can bore their friends about for years. Twenty-five inches, more. Every morning there's a line of drift boats at the landing, a nightmare scenario. I would rather fish with nobody around, who wouldn't? But I love this river and I want to fish with my friend Todd, who guides down there. And who knows, maybe we'll get lucky at the end of the year.

On the drive down from New York there's fall color, a wall of deep yellow, along the entire Shenandoah Ridge. Exits on the highway point toward Civil War battlefields. Signs remind you that Virginia is for lovers. There's something about fishing in the South that fascinates me. It feels improbable, the landscape is brooding and gothic. It may be my imagination but it feels mistier and evocative.

I'm staying near Bristol, Tennessee, which shares a main street with Bristol, Virginia. Bristol is one of the only cities in America that's in two different states. Todd has arranged for me to stay in a wood cabin with a stone fireplace on the porch. After the long drive—through seven states—I make a fire and think about the fishing. Even in the dark I can make out the river through the trees.

Todd is the only guide I've met who has attended divinity school. This is not something he discusses. *A River Runs Through It* begins with the famous line "In our family, there was no clear line between religion and fly fishing." Todd, unlike Norman Maclean, keeps an angling separation of church and state. Todd has other intriguing secrets. There's a *How to Learn Italian* CD in the back seat of his truck, not something commonly found among a guide's fly boxes. Todd is meticulous in a way I find reassuring. Like many successful guides he has a low-key approach to client acquisition. He fishes with people he likes or are referred by his friends. I feel good to have passed the test.

The morning is cold as we set up in Todd's boat. Then we move below all the drift boats by the dam to have a little breathing room. As I mentioned, and it can't really be mentioned enough, there are alarmingly large trout in this river. Brown trout at this size become true predators. They no longer just look for nymphs, stone flies, and grasshoppers. They also stalk minnows, mice, frogs, small fish, and fish that aren't that small. They feed at night. They play the long game, wait very still, sometimes for hours, then ambush some poor critter.

This is the fish we want to catch. Though they prefer something substantial, they still eat small nymphs. Very small. The size of a grape seed. Why would a big fish eat something so small? Well it doesn't just eat one. It eats a hundred. Like when you destroy a bag of popcorn before the previews end. You get into a routine and the fish does too. You want your nymph to look like every other nymph and you want the fish to react reflexively. Nymph. Nymph. Nymph. Your nymph. And there you are ready to triumph.

But it's not as easy as that. Nothing ever is. Setting a trout on a small nymph is a delicate business. When a trout takes a nymph the angler rarely feels it. So anglers put a strike indicator on the line, basically a bobber, and if that bobber plunges or moves suddenly, then raise the rod to set the hook. Do this quickly because the fish will realize that something is strange, open its mouth, and your chance is over. Often the angler is blissfully unaware. But sometimes it's not blissful because the angler suspects he may have had a fish and lost it. And any lost unseen fish will be presumed large. I know, anglers, we're exhausting.

This morning there are no bugs on the surface, so we hope our fish will take a nymph. Todd sets up a double nymph rig that's pretty gnarly. There's no artistry involved here, no majestic casting. Just get your nymphs out there, throw in a mend, get a good drift, and be patient. This is what you use to catch one fish you *really* want to catch. You have to cast slowly or they'll get tangled and you have to tie the whole thing again and it's a big mess. The guide pulls the boat over while you sit, like a misbehaving student in a time-out, and he sets up your rig as boats pass by and you look like an absolute clown. Everybody knows what you did.

It's early and we're talking about the last few years and I'm enjoying being back on the South Holston. The sun is just up. I'm barely in the game when the white bobber disappears. I raise the rod. A hard set. There's no telltale movement of the trout's head. It's absolutely solid. The boat moves downstream and the nymph stays where it is. We're in deeper water with a fast current as Todd starts to row upstream to fight the fish. Still it doesn't move. After a few seconds I urge it, slightly *urge* it toward us. I exert a small amount of pressure, repeat *small amount of pressure*. Mistake.

The line goes slack and everything becomes clear. Like when they reveal the murderer in the final scene of a BBC mystery. Oh the surly butler! His heart full of resentment. I should have known! Todd shudders slightly and is honest enough to say, "That was the fish." I'm quiet for a second. "It didn't move," I say, trying out a possible line of defense. Todd smiles a little uneasily. "No, they don't move." How can the fish we've been looking for arrive five minutes after we started while it's still freezing out?

I need another approach. "Maybe it was a rock?" I ask. "I'm not sure there are rocks that far out," Todd politely eviscerates this premise. The old rock excuse. Have I learned nothing? Never blame a rock. Humiliating. So what should I have done? Todd explains that you have to let the trout sit after it's hooked. Then, suddenly, it will bolt downstream and we'll follow it in the boat. Wow. That was news to me.

But it shouldn't have been because I didn't follow one of my basic rules. When you start fishing with a guide, talk about how to handle the dream scenario. I appreciate that planning for a big fish invites bad luck, but you have to be prepared. Sometimes guides presume I know what I'm doing. Wrong! "There are no classes for beginners in life; the most difficult thing is always asked of one right away." Those wise words are from the famous trout angler Rilke. No, he didn't fish, but the sentiment remains true.

I secretly think this will end any big fish dreams on the South Holston. I sense Todd does too. We float for a few hours and nothing much happens. But we have another plan. Just as the sun sets, which is early at this time of year, there's a Yellow Sally stone-fly hatch. This is much nicer than using a double nymph rig. We wade and rainbows are rising and I catch a few. Bright silver fish, with the wide rose stripes. It's always nice to catch trout as the sun goes down.

The light reflects on the water and it's an easygoing setting. Then there's a surge of water near the far bank. A beaver? The action is abrupt. Now there are stories about immense trout in the South Holston. Like all fish stories I meet them halfway. "That's one of the big fish," Todd says and raises his eyebrows. What? "It's chasing a smaller fish." That was an aggressive move. A feeding move. I'm concerned. "If it's chasing a fish will it still take a Yellow Sally?" I ask. Todd measures his words. "It will if you put the fly right in front of it."

I was not expecting things to escalate so quickly. I should let that large trout settle down. I work my way over and see a log where the trout would naturally lie. I cast a few times. It's hard to stay calm knowing that fish could be right there. Every movement feels like it's the trout. None of them are. That's a fish people name. That's a fish you plan your life around. We'll try again tomorrow.

Back at Todd's truck he pours bourbon in a small round

glass. "This is how we serve bourbon in our family." It's an old jam jar. Nice. The bourbon is so good I don't ask for more. This is how to end a day down South.

Don't argue with southerners about college football and don't argue with them about barbecue. Ridgewood Barbecue in Bluff City is full at lunch on a weekday afternoon. I wouldn't say it's in a remote location though it's probably an hour from the nearest building with an elevator. The house specialty, which they've served since 1948, is a smoked pork sandwich, *Tennessee Style*, with a recipe known only by two members of the founding family. Barbecue secrets are as closely held as angling secrets. Oh and there's coleslaw, quite light, served on Saltines. And sweet tea in an enormous plastic cup. Any questions?

There are framed old covers of *Sports Illustrated* on the wall from the Volunteers' glory days, the color starting to fade. I eat half my lunch and bring the rest home for dinner by the fire.

Todd and I float down the Holston again but we don't entice any large trout. It's just not happening. So we ditch the boat and return to where we waded yesterday. Now Todd's fishing with me. The fish are rising all the way to the bank as the sun goes down. This is also like Spain in that you focus nearby. That's a universal rule, but I like comparing things to how they were in Spain.

I watch Todd fish. He's methodical and never hurries.

Every good angler I've seen is relaxed when they cast. They don't do anything dramatic unless they have to. Once, Todd does miss a bigger fish and swears, which I find encouraging. Though he may have done that just to make me feel better.

I focus on making the best cast I can while still controlling the drift. Increasingly, the drift is my primary concern. A perfectly placed cast won't do much unless there's a natural drift. There are fewer insects out tonight but there are still rises and we catch fish and Todd catches larger ones. Funny how that happens.

There's no sign of the fish from yesterday. But just knowing that it prowls the area is exciting. It could be anywhere. There's a time on the water, late in the day, when you realize the dream is not going to happen. Nobody comments on it, but everybody knows. This doesn't have to be bad, in a way the pressure's gone. You enjoy the evening light and the rising trout and are happy to catch anything before the day ends.

The next morning I get up early. Todd is back on the river guiding his next sports. Life on the South Holston continues without me. I drive back to New York and take a detour to Charlottesville, to a dive restaurant that's not as good as I remember. Or maybe it was never that good but just has a good name. The sky is gray and the leaves, even after a few days, are already starting to fall.

Fall in New York seems to get shorter every year. I drive up to the Catskills and the trees are brighter as I head north. I'm fishing with my friend Darrell who moved up from the city during the pandemic. Darrell lives in Livingston Manor, in Sullivan County, an area with fly fishing history. Darrell is a writer, thoughtful, and more measured than most of my friends. I wonder about the change from Manhattan. "It feels very natural," he says. We feel a certain sympathy. Our significant others are less enthused with country life than we are. His wife often works in New York or Los Angeles. Is it hard? "It's a balance. We try to find the right amount of time in the country and the city." Of course the right amount of time is not always agreed upon. We don't dwell on these matters, we're here to fish after all. But standing by the water is a good place to reflect.

We're on a stream where I fish often, so Darrell has most of the action. Darrell appreciates tradition and is not afraid to smoke his grandfather's pipe. The pipe is one of the last and least explored affectations. I admire Darrell's verve and it suits him well, in a 1920s explorer way. His family's summer house in Maine has no power, so that gives you some pipe-smoking cover.

Now Darrell can fish every day. Sometimes he'll text me in the city and say that there's a great hatch, that I should come up. *Lots of fish rising.* He just walks outside and casts. The city equivalent is passing a popular restaurant with an empty table and going right in. There will always be a desire to live near the water. That matters enough to people so they do something about it. The rest of us try to find time to head out into the world and make our own luck.

When I'm in the city I imagine life in the country, especially when the fishing is good. Of course, when you're in the country you might pick up a *New York Times* and read about some exhibition or miss the feeling of going to a bar where you know the staff. There's no perfect equation.

On the water, I like serving as an informal guide. Darrell casts well so it's even nicer. "Try by the rock," I tell him. "They sometimes hold where the water comes through that channel." He puts his fly on the spot and a fish comes and takes it. He lands a lovely brown trout, the darkest black spots standing out against the gold body. This is why we're here. "Thanks for the guidance." We both know he would have cast there anyway, but it's nice to have the illusion of giving sage advice. I feel powerful even though Darrell did all the work. Is this what being an executive producer is like?

I keep thinking about what it would be like to live near a river. How closely you would appreciate the changes every day. It's hard enough to navigate life on your own and even more delicate with another person. There are always sacrifices, there's no other way. How do we want to live? What are we willing to give up? Late in the afternoon Darrell and I have moved beyond life analysis for the day. We follow the bend in the stream and it's quiet on the water as the sun goes down behind the bluff.

Driving back I take a detour to a river where I haven't fished in a long time. The Housatonic. This is Litchfield County, Connecticut. You can see the water from Route 7, and you cross over on a covered bridge. Turn left on the dirt road before the train tracks, it goes down a hill and turns to run along the river. You'll see red signs posted to trees with white block letters reading ALL TROUT MUST BE RETURNED WITHOUT AVOIDABLE INJURY. A good mantra.

I started fishing this river over twenty years ago. I can't believe it's been that long. I came to this area with a painter and his wife, who had a lovely farmhouse downstream on the other side of the small town. At that point I hadn't fished often for trout, especially in large rivers, much less on my own. All of which is to say: I had only the vaguest idea what I was doing.

Despite my struggles, I loved to fish on that river. I would come up for the weekend, and Saturday afternoons he would paint, she would garden, and I'd catch a trout or two, if I was lucky. And it really was luck. I would usually catch a bass, by accident, as my first fish of the season. There's a specific disappointment to the trout angler as a fish comes closer and turns out to be a bass. Like drinking a nonalcoholic beer by mistake.

I was younger than my hosts, like their nephew. They lived beautifully in a house full of books and paintings and cats named after favorite artists. One year when the water was low, I waded across the entire river to catch one large rising fish, a rare unalloyed Housatonic triumph. I walked back through a mowed path in the field to my car and changed out of my waders on the dirt road. I've always loved passing through fields after a good day on the water. Everything seems designed for you, a wink from the gods.

Once my car keys fell out of a hole in a new rain jacket that shouldn't have had any holes. They were lost in the river, long gone. I walked back to the house in my waders, more than a mile, arriving just as the dinner guests did. "Catch anything?" they asked in unison. This was my Saab era. It turned out re-cutting the key was easy. But the Swedes, in a classic move of overthinking, required the installation of an ignition box that would recognize the new key. This protected Saab owners from thieves who were presumably cutting keys to try to steal Saabs from NPR listeners around New England. The box cost a thousand dollars. The company apologized, and gave me a generous credit. They stopped making that wading jacket. Anyway, that's the car I ended up trading for a fishing rod. The cycle continues.

And it really does continue. In recent years the painter and I grew apart. The reasons are general and specific, like all gently fraying friendships. People get older, their habits change, the uncle/nephew dynamic can't be maintained. Who can say? He died, suddenly, this summer. Like all his friends, I was devastated. Some deaths wash over you like a flash flood.

Standing here now, I think of him. It's out of season, the water's brown and uninviting. The trees are stark. I realize that I've grown apart from this water. Relationships with rivers change too. You form new habits, fish a different way, head farther afield. When you return the feeling isn't the same. Today, in the aftermath of everything that happened, the water fails to reassure me. Rivers move to their own time, as they always have. We simply pass through the greater story.

Standing on the Housatonic I think back to time I spent in this area. Summer arrived, the lawns were so green, the air felt heavy and it was welcome to wade out into the river, getting cooler with every step. Coming to this river, staying at this house, being with these friends, was a major part of my life, and I hope, in a smaller way, of their lives too.

You mark your life by the people and places you know. And some of us start to mark our lives by fish. The first trout on a fly. The first bonefish on your own. The first time you felt in control of the process. You realize how little you knew way back when. You might feel tenderly toward your younger, inexperienced self. Yes, fishing becomes a thread of your triumphs and setbacks, which, when looked at this way, are not so fleeting after all.

In moments of success you and the fish come together on the bank in a rare moment of intimacy. We are opposites, each living where the other cannot. I'm always struck by the beauty of fish, but especially trout. When they're in the net I look at their eye, fierce and black, staring past me, and feel cut with shame. This fish provided a thrill by behaving naturally. I don't linger. I rarely take photos, I try not to take the fish out of the water. Sometimes the fish will rest in the shallows while it recovers. I watch until it swims away and dissolves into its mysterious world.

Sometimes I'm embarrassed when I remember the intense thrill catching a fish gave me. That's unfair. How do you discount youthful enthusiasm? Of course you're excited in the moment. You'll never love a band like your first band. And you'll never love a fish like your first fish. Maybe one reason I keep fishing new rivers in new places is to recapture that feeling. Maybe. But maybe I just love to be on the water.

AFTERWORD

THE LONG WAY HOME

It's November in the Catskills. I'm alone. It's cold and I make a fire in the small wooden cabin. This is the last time I'll fish this year. What began in Patagonia in January is ending in Upstate New York before Thanksgiving. Without the leaves on the trees you sense the true contours of the landscape and see the stream more clearly. The water is brisk. The fish are wary.

Fishing, when you've done it enough, starts to form a continuum, a collapsed timeline of experience and memory. When you return to the water in the beginning of the season you're connected to the previous year and every time you've been on the water. The intervening months drift away and you bring back memories, some of them self-serving. I've yet to meet an angler who's reluctant to point toward the pool where he once triumphed. He remembers it with the clarity of first love. You can step into the same fishing story twice.

Fishing late into the fall adds another chapter to the season. Because I fish here often I feel less urgency. Could I bring this more tranquil approach to new destinations? Could I remain calm and keep perspective? Probably not. Part of what makes a fishing trip exciting is that it's self-contained. Knowing the days will end creates a certain intensity. The same way visiting a city will always be different than living there. I'd like to be mellow. But do I really want to care less?

Years ago, when I started fishing more and more, I sensed where this would lead. I knew it could consume part of my life. I developed a fascination with what it would take to break the fever. I would design a plan—say, fish for one hundred days straight—that would theoretically cure this obsession. I never carried these plans out, of course. The idea was just to speculate about what would finally be enough. Then I could retire and return to a normal life. That never happened. I'm not sure it works like that, anyway. The only people I know who've given up fishing usually moved on to something just as specific, like building wooden boats.

Did I think, on some level, that this year would break the fever? I'm not sure. In any case, it didn't. Nothing diminished my desire to be on the water. If anything I'm ready to go back to Norway for a month. Who knows, maybe I'll visit Johan. Fishing is still in my system. That won't change. I do think I've arrived at a better balance, based on something I already knew: You can survive very well with less fishing, or anything else for that matter. You'll be all right.

When it's cold the fish don't get active until the sun is on the stream and the water warms up. That's late in the morning or early afternoon. They conserve their energy and move slowly. I certainly do. When it's forty degrees everything feels more elemental. Maybe because it's the last fishing of the year, maybe because my fingers are freezing.

It's natural to be philosophical in November. The days are getting shorter. The landscape doesn't hide behind the leaves. I'd like to have some concise wisdom that will be applicable to your life as well as mine. Ideally we can all come out ahead here. Unfortunately, that, in my experience, is not the way wisdom works. There's no short cut, no self-help book, no retreat, no guru, no mountaintop, no fad diet, no hack, no money-back guarantee. What's worth knowing can only be found the long way.

The premise of fly fishing is the same wherever you are. The specifics are different, certainly, but you're hoping to convince something living to eat something that's not living. Then you reel it in. It's in our nature to escalate things and hard to keep simple things simple. So we go further. Catch bigger fish. Lose the biggest fish. Cross into Ahab territory. These impulses are not new. And they'll continue after we're gone.

All anglers romanticize better, earlier times. You should have been there, the old timers say, the fish were so large, the rivers undiscovered. Those were the days and we'll never go back. We know this. Today, the numbers are down everywhere, and they'll continue to go down. It's strange and sad to think that fifty years from now people will look back to our time and think how lucky we've been. We're left to navigate the tension between the beauty of the world and knowing the way it actually works.

And yet we are lucky. It's easy to lose a sense of wonder and, even at this age, I don't want to lose that sense. Maybe that's why I keep trying to find it. I still consider catching a fish you've always wanted, in a traditional way, to be a worthy pursuit. The success will not solve things forever. Nothing ever does. That's the danger with getting what you want—you have to find something else to dream about.

I cast again in the cold. Not a brilliant cast. The best anglers possess skills I'll never have. I remain an enthusiastic amateur and in the end that will have to be that. I may approach a few moments of grace, but I'll always know that there's a more rarified version of what I try to do. The time it will take to graduate is something I'll never have unless I leave this life behind. I'm not prepared to take a monk's oath for the water. Maybe that's why I admire those who make the time. They have a discipline, or a disregard for domesticity, that I don't have. There's a divide between those who go all the way and those who witness expertise and imitate it, but still keep a foot in their civilian life.

AFTERWORD

The same way I admire those who move to a farmhouse in a remote Italian valley. I'm attracted to that impulse and frightened by it. Do they have the secret? Do they, in their pastoral lives, have regrets?

On this stream I take my time. Returning to beloved pools and well-known bends is a great legacy. The gravity in our world speeds everything up. Fly fishing, in its best form, will always be slower, and thank goodness it will never be efficient. A small brown trout speeds to the surface from a deep pool and takes my fly. A lively fish. It surprises me. I hadn't expected action, if I'm honest. The trout is bright, a shining silver. Beneath the clouds, the red spots look even more vivid. I release the trout and it swims back down, a burst of light, impossibly vital, disappearing into the darkness. Being close to such a fine creature, perfect in its way, makes me feel alive in the cold.

Do you live your life in far-off places? Do you stay close to home? These desires wax, they wane. In the stream above me water cascades down over large rocks, the only sound I can hear. The fish is safe below, out of sight. The last trout of the year. In the moment, on this gray day, this feels like enough.

ACKNOWLEDGMENTS

Creating a book is a curiously asymmetrical process. It is, by turn, intensely solitary, then quickly involves a lot of people, all experts in their field. It's important to put yourself in good hands when you come out the other side. I consider myself lucky to work with these fine people in the publishing world.

Elias Altman. Agent, strategist, wise counsel and friend. I'm incredibly indebted to you.

Colin Harrison. Every writer needs to trust their editor and that's easy when he's thoughtful, humane, and politely skeptical. Countless thanks to the rest of the wonderful team at Scribner: Nan Graham, Emily Polson, Brian Belfiglio, Mark LaFlaur, Stuart Smith, Jaya Miceli, Jaime Putorti, Yvonne Taylor, Annie Craig, Mark Galarrita, Brianna Yamashita, and Alexis Seabrook for her great illustrations.

John Gall, who's designed a wonderful cover (this makes four books we've worked on together). Wanting to see what you come up with makes me want to make it to the end.

This book involved worldwide logistics, from guides to lodges to cars. Thanks to my friends at Patagonia River Guides, Travis Smith, Rance Rathie, Alex Knüll. Also: John Sugden. Turtle Inn. The good people at Volvo, Russell Datz, Lars Walker, Magnus Holst, and Hans Hedberg.

ACKNOWLEDGMENTS

Thomas McGuane, Sam Sifton, Chris Dombrowski, Jay McInerney, Peter Kaminsky, Tom Rosenbauer, all anglers and writers of a high order, who've helped along the way. Paul Croughton, for encouraging my writing on fishing when I was just getting into the game. Also: JP Smith. Charles McGrath. Michael Williams.

My fishing friends, who are of course more than that: Markley Boyer, Matt Hranek, Ruaridh Nicoll, Norman Vilalta, Darrell Hartman, Taite Pearson, Todd Hare, Mike Idell, Joel Stoehr, Brendan McCarthy, Mungo Ingleby, Peter Treichel, Finlay Wilson, Verlon Herndon, and Takahiro Osaki.

My family of delightful angling agnostics: David, Wendy, and Sarah Coggins. How do you separate anything you make from the way you grew up and learned to live?

Most importantly, to Emilie Hawtin. A book is nothing compared to a life together. And that life, more than anything else, will always matter most.

ABOUT THE AUTHOR

David Coggins is the author of *The Optimist: A Case for the Fly Fishing Life* and the *New York Times* bestseller *Men and Style*. He writes *The Contender* newsletter, and his work has appeared in numerous publications, including the *Financial Times*, *Esquire*, and *Condé Nast Traveler*. Coggins lives in New York and fishes regularly in the Catskills and Montana.